Christian
Set Yourself Free

by

Graham and Shirley Powell

New Wine Press

Unless otherwise stated, Scripture quotations in this volume are from the New American Standard Bible,©The Lockman Foundation, 1960, 1962, 1963, 1968, 1971, 1972, 1973, 1975, La Habra, California.

Other Scripture quotations are from the Amplified New Testament (AMP),©The Lockman Foundation 1954, 1958; and from the Authorized Version (AV).

First published 1983
British edition 1986

New Wine Press
P.O. Box 17
Chichester
England

ISBN 0 947852 17 4

Acknowledgments

To Rev. Noel and Mrs. Phyl Gibson who started us on the road to freedom and whose love and guidance strengthened us during the most difficult period of our lives.

To Roseann Barnes whose dedication to the task of editing and typing the manuscript has played a major part in the preparation of this book.

The authors regret, that because of their extensive commitments, they are unable to offer personal counselling services.

iv

About the Authors

Graham and Shirley Powell were born in New Zealand and raised in Presbyterian and Open Brethren homes respectively. Graham was an elementary teacher and Shirley a typist and book-keeper before they moved into evangelistic ministry. Shirley is a songwriter and sister of David Garratt of Scripture in Song Recordings. Her songs have been sung worldwide for many years. For a period of ten years they worked with an interdenominational evangelistic organization, based in Wellington and Hamilton, New Zealand, and then in Sydney and Parkes, Australia.

Moving to Brisbane, Australia, Graham became an Associate Pastor, and Shirley, Director of Music, in an inner-city church. In 1980 they settled in Canada and continued in pastoral work on the Coast and then in the Interior of British Columbia. They have two children. Currently they are involved in evangelistic and teaching ministry in Canada and beyond.

Graham and Shirley Powell conduct teaching seminars and deliverance and healing meetings.

Enquiries as to the availability of their ministry should be directed to:

Center Mountain Ministries,
P.O. Box 120
Westbridge,
B.C. VOH 2BO
Canada.

Contents

Chapter 1

Crisis and Quest

Shirley and I had come to a crisis, but little did we realize that out of it events were to unfold that would revolutionize our lives.

For some years I had been an evangelist in an interdenominational organization, but in the work problems persisted to which there seemed to be no solution. Frustrated, and lacking in maturity, I had handed my resignation to the national director.

"What guidance have you had from the Lord to make this decision?" my director asked as I sat in his office. We talked for several hours, and eventually I concluded that God had not guided us to leave.

Then turning the conversation, he asked, "Graham, do you have any personal problems that you would like to share with me?"

Personal problems! It seemed to me my life was full of problems. Outwardly I was a zealous servant of God, yet inwardly I struggled with great needs. There were many areas of my life in which I lacked freedom and victory, although I had sought answers for years. For hours daily, I had prayed and cried to God for help, but had remained unchanged.

Problems? Yes! But could my director help? Over the years I had sought counsel from many leading ministers in the Body of Christ, but after pouring out my heart, the answer was always the same: "I'm sorry, I can't help you."

Could I receive help now? Would I have to humiliate myself again by confessing deep areas of need and finding no relief? In the present situation there was little choice; so once again I shared.

My director listened, and then offered to pray for me, saying that he felt the source of my conflicts were evil spirits, and that I needed deliverance. Not wanting to face further disappointment, I was reluctant to accept his offer, but left promising to think it over.

Deciding to accept his help, we gathered with our wives and

began seeking the Lord. Then suddenly it happened! Something inside me manifested with tremendous strength and pressure. Never before had this happened! An inward power gripped me intensely and I began to shake. My immediate reaction was one of fear. Something began to cry out through my lips as my friends commanded release in Jesus' name.

Fear — yes; but also hope. At the same time that fear gripped me, I found myself saying within: "When this power is broken, I'm going to be different! I'll be changed! Something other than myself has caused me to be the way I've been."

For the first time I realized that evil spirits were the source of my problems. There was no doubting it.

Thoughts of hope were filling my mind: "When tonight is over, I'll be free! I'll tell the world about this! I'll open the eyes of God's people! I'll tell them Jesus can be their Deliverer! Tomorrow, I'll . . . ."

Four hours later I lay on the floor exhausted and disappointed. There had been great stirrings, but no release. Another time for prayer was set aside. Again it ended in disappointment. Session after session followed. The results were always the same.

My director and his wife were at a loss. They had prayed for many people in this way and seen great results. Never had they met a situation like mine. Why could they help others, but not me? I began to think back over my life. There were several incidents that came readily to mind that could have given entry to evil spirits. But what hindered them from leaving? Neither I nor those with me knew.

I had been brought up in New Zealand in a home that believed in Christian principles. Our family attended the local Presbyterian Church. As a child my heart had been open to God, and at the age of six I asked Jesus to come into my life. However, within days of this decision, I experienced an onslaught of the enemy — a counterattack to the cry of my heart (not that I recognized it as such then). Through no fault of my own, an incident occurred which literally overwhelmed me with fear. Through this, the enemy established a major stronghold within me. From that day on, my mind was constantly filled with fears, and often the grip of fear made my body stiff and tense. I had to learn to live with this.

In my teen years the fears increased, but in spite of this I continued to be an outgoing person actively involved in many school activities including the Christian group in which I became the student leader. Near the end of high school I organized the school dance. This conflicted with the standards of the other Christian leaders. I had learned to dance at church and saw nothing wrong with it. Considering them narrow-minded, I resigned and ceased to fellowship with them, choosing instead the company of the world. Looking back, this decision led to further deception and opened the door to much greater demonic infiltration.

Leaving high school, I joined the merchant navy. To go to sea had always been my ambition. Unfortunately, it brought me into the company of men who had no respect for God or Christian principles. For some months I walked a so-called Christian pathway before succumbing to the pressures of the environment. I turned away from the Lord and even began to curse the name of Christ. My fears continued to increase, and I was engulfed by depression, self-pity, and loneliness. A lifelong allergy caused constant breathing difficulties. The fulfillment I had sought through a life at sea had evaded me.

Coming ashore I began to train as a school teacher. I also played the saxophone and joined a dance band. I looked forward to the balls and the Saturday night engagements. There was excitement for a period, but it never lasted. An emptiness inside could not be filled. It was then that I considered going back to church.

Glancing at a newspaper, I saw a youth crusade scheduled in the local opera house. The speaker was to be an evangelist from the U.S.A. He led a musical team and had been a professional musician before becoming a preacher. The music attracted me to the meetings.

The first night he spoke on the second coming of Jesus Christ when He would judge mankind. I had not heard this message before. As I listened, I was greatly convicted of sin. As a child I had opened my heart to Christ, but now God seemed so far away. Darkness surrounded me. I heard again of Jesus coming to earth the first time to bear away my sin; of His rising from the dead; of His returning to heaven; and now of His ultimate return to earth in judgment.

God was speaking to me. He was giving me another opportunity to turn to Him — perhaps the last. I knew it had to be a total response, an all or nothing decision. Choosing to give everything to Jesus, I lifted up my heart to God and uttered a deep cry of repentance; I asked forgiveness for my sin, and acknowledged Jesus Christ as Lord.

When I finished praying, the preacher's voice was still sounding. But something had happened. I felt clean; I knew I had been forgiven; assurance of eternal life filled my heart; I knew I was going to heaven, not hell; Jesus was alive to me! After the meeting I

3

remember thinking: "Now I know God. Now I have someone to turn to, someone to help me out of my problems."

A new course had been set — a turning from the old ways. Now Jesus Christ was central in my life; His will was paramount. The Bible became a living book, and Christian fellowship was wonderful. Constantly I witnessed to the reality of forgiveness and of knowing God personally. Loneliness left and the depression eased considerably. However, the fears persisted and the breathing difficulties were the same. I began to ask God to set me free completely.

As the weeks went by, my hunger for God grew. One day a Christian friend spoke to me about being baptized in the Holy Spirit. This too was new to me, but I gladly responded to the truth of God's Word. The following night Jesus baptized me in His Spirit. I was overwhelmed with a new sense of His presence, a new reality to His Word, a new desire to praise Him, a new joy, and a new power for service. For a week I lived in the clouds, but then came to earth again. To my disappointment the old problems were still there. True, a new release had come, but deep inside I was still crying for answers.

Soon after this I had an unusual experience. The Lord had been challenging me about spending more time with Him, and I had not fully responded. Right at that time I went to a church where the visiting preacher challenged the congregation on spending time in God's presence. As he spoke, it seemed as if his eyes became glued to mine. Bright rays of light came from his eyes and beamed in upon me. The light was brighter than any earthly light. I felt exposed to God. He was searching my heart. Such was the intensity of the light, I instinctively ducked low behind the seat in front. The preacher continued speaking obviously unaware how God had used him to speak to me. My obedience to this challenge was to be my source of strength for the new pressures that were to come. Without this obedience, I could not have endured the years that were to follow.

In the vacation at the end of my teacher training course, an invitation came to play the saxophone in a musical team at a beach mission. It was here that I first met Shirley Garratt, the young lady who was to become my wife. The following year I took a teaching position.

As time went on, especially since being baptized in the Holy Spirit, I was noticing a strange contrast. In some ways my life was becoming better and better; and yet in other ways, it was becoming worse and worse. Although growing spiritually, and vitally involved in Christian service, my fears were becoming more intense. Bouts of deep depression, that would take days to come out of, gripped me. During these bouts, pressures to commit suicide plagued me, and worry intensified. Looking back, I now understand why this was: The Holy Spirit had been released to work in my life in a new measure, and this brought an increased stirring from the hidden demonic strongholds.

Outwardly, no one knew of these pressures. It seemed the more I followed Jesus, the harder it became. Every positive blessing and desire was being contrasted by negative ones. This pattern was to continue for years. Waiting on God daily was the only thing that gave me strength to continue living. My times in prayer increased until I averaged around four hours a day. It was not that I always wanted to pray and read the Word for such lengthy periods, but to maintain inner strength, I was forced to.

The bouts of depression continued. I discovered the only way to break them was by days of prayer and fasting. This pattern also was to continue for years.

Determined to break free from the inner turmoils, I resigned from teaching so that I could seek God in an even more intense way. (Never once did I imagine needing deliverance from evil spirits.) Going to a farm on a small island off the coast of New Zealand, I began to seek the Lord in prayer and fasting. I had determined not to break the fast until I was free. This didn't work — and neither did it work at any later time. Because of my health, I was forced to break the fast. However, I stayed and continued to seek the Lord.

While I was there, a young man visited the farm and prophesied over me on more than one occasion that by a certain date, some weeks ahead, I would be set free. Believing this to be a word from God, my expectation for healing and freedom increased as the foretold date approached. It came and went, dashing my expectations to the ground. I learned through this that people can prophesy from their own hearts. What a serious thing to say, "Thus saith the Lord," and then speak in the flesh!

After three months, I reluctantly returned to the mainland. Fortunately, I never became bitter against God, even though it seemed He did not answer my deep cries and my many tears. I just continued on, disappointed.

Moving to the city of Wellington, I became involved as a voluntary worker with an evangelistic organization. Shirley was also a team member, and during this time our friendship deepened, and the following year we were married.

5

With the inward pressures continuing, I sought the counsel of various ministers. Time and time again I poured out my heart asking for help, but received none. No one seemed to understand what I was going through or how to help me. If any word summed up my life, it was TORMENT. Continually I lived in torment. The only relief I had was when I fasted and prayed. But because I had to eat to live, fasting could only give temporary relief.

Six months after we were married, our keenness to serve God led us into full-time evangelistic ministry, first in New Zealand, then in Australia. How difficult it was to serve the Lord! It is one thing to have inner needs; but it is another thing to be on the front line preaching to the unsaved — still with inner needs. Preparing messages was a battle. My mind was continually distracted. I could not relax. Tension was my experience day and night. I was so tense that I couldn't patiently wait at the kitchen sink for dishes to be washed and placed in the drying tray; I had to be active or seeking God. For years our social life was restricted. If we were asked to go out for a meal a few days in advance, I was reluctant to commit myself because I didn't know how I would be feeling. If the day had been good, I could endure the evening; if bad, it would be agony.

In my seeking I read many books. I tried to apply principles in Christian psychology, but they either didn't work or I couldn't do what they said. Knowing the importance of living in God's Word, I memorized a thousand Bible verses. I did all I knew: prayed, read the Word, walked in obedience, gave tithes and offerings, fasted regularly, went out on altar calls to be prayed for by others; but nothing broke the inward pressures.

I was maintaining my Christian walk only by daily waiting on God and being renewed and strengthened. This was keeping me going, but not conquering my inner needs. Heaven seemed my only hope. I longed for the end of my earthly pilgrimage when I would be free from my earthly body and all its inner conflicts. I longed for escape.

*   *   *   *

But now a crisis had come! In the presence of my director, the enemy's work had been exposed for what it was: I was bound by evil spirits. However, again my hopes of freedom had come crashing down in disappointment. I was in demonic bondage, but how could I get free? Hours and hours of praying! My counselors perplexed! How desperate I became!

6

I continued to fulfill my normal evangelistic duties, and the amazing thing was that the Lord blessed them. Even though all hell had broken loose within me, souls continued to be saved. Few knew of my struggles. I fasted. I prayed. I cried to God with my whole heart. What more could I do?

Not only had my director and our wives prayed for me, others had been called in. A minister from a large church in Europe had been asked to talk with me. He assured me strongly that Christians could not be bound by demons because once we were born of God's Spirit, we were set free. After the violent manifestations I had experienced, his words did not impress me — nor my director. We knew I needed deliverance. He had no alternate solution to offer.

Another minister who had had dealings with the demon-possessed on an Asian mission field was approached. He also tried to persuade me I wasn't bound by demons and suggested I read Deuteronomy 28 which speaks of blessings through obedience and cursings through disobedience. But that was no comfort. Since turning my life completely over to Jesus Christ, I had endeavored to walk closely with Him, continually choosing the way of obedience. How could I be cursed for disobedience?

Perhaps a psychiatrist could help? A specialist had graciously offered to see me without cost. I drove my gospel van to his consulting rooms. In gold letters on each side of the vehicle was written: CHRIST DIED FOR OUR SINS. I felt so ashamed I parked a few houses away. How exhausted I was! On top of everything, I had been having restless nights with horrible dreams. Reluctantly, I sat before his desk. I was serving a Christ who had all-power; One who had defeated Satan. Why should I have to seek answers from such a source? Yet, I was grateful for someone who perhaps could help.

"What treatment would you like me to give you?" he asked after we had talked for a while. His question took me by surprise. He then outlined eight alternate treatments of which I remember only three: taking L.S.D., shock treatment, and hypnotherapy. Frankly, none appealed to me. I told him I was in his hands and preferred he made the decision.

Hypnotherapy was his choice. In this area he was highly qualified. But somehow I sensed it was not right for a Christian. As I lay on his couch, I lifted up my heart to the Lord asking His protection if it would harm me in any way. (I did not know then that hypnotherapy is part of occult practice.) He tried on three occasions to hypnotize me, but without success. I was not resisting, but in my desperation was crying out to God for help and protection. At the end of the third attempt, I heard again the all-too-familiar reply: "I'm sorry, I can't help you." I received a prescription for further sedatives, and that was that.

Was there an answer? Would I ever be changed? How long could I keep serving God under such tremendous inward pressures?

It was not until three months had passed, and forty hours of praying were behind us, that the first releasing came. Another minister had been consulted, and another time of prayer arranged. First one session, then another, and finally on the third, the break came. As always there were great manifestations and tearings within, but no obvious release. After a time, however, the team praying all sensed that a measure of deliverance had taken place. I didn't feel or notice anything, but they were sure God had done something. They had been praying against the source of my breathing difficulties. Ever since a child, pollen, dust, or any slight change of temperature in a room would start me sneezing. I usually spent the first hours of every day with congested sinuses. Often I suffered all day long. Now, although I was still congested and felt no different, I was told deliverance had taken place. Two mornings later I awoke delighted to find that I was breathing clearly. No congestion. No sneezing. I was thrilled! At last there was evidence that God was breaking the enemy's power. I was healed and still am healed these many years later.

Soon after this, we were transferred within our work to a new location with new responsibilities. It was a step in God's purposes, but it took us away from regular close fellowship with our director and his wife. They felt that for the time being, they had helped us as much as they were able to. However, although the Lord had touched one area of my life, my deepest needs were still not met. It was to be a further five years of searching, praying, and fasting before I learned to understand the work of the enemy and to cooperate with God to minister deliverance to myself. They were five years of continuing struggles in which I often felt I could no longer continue in the ministry.

Amazingly, the years became increasingly fruitful. The Lord prospered us in many ways that we never sought or coveted after. Souls continued to be saved, and by every outward appearance we could have been registered as "successful" in our field of endeavor. Yet the inward pressures continued. There was never a let-up day or night. As always, I spent hours daily in seeking God, crying for release; but the bondages remained. Into my hands came literature

8

and tapes on demon-possession, but none helped me to obtain freedom. All majored on the work of the enemy, but none on how to break free. They usually expressed a prayer of renunciation of Satan's works. I would pray the prayer, but nothing would happen. Thankfully, just ahead was a turning point.

For some time we were being prepared by the Holy Spirit to take a new step in our lives. Many years of service within the organization we served had passed. We longed to be free to preach Bible truths that we could not preach because of organizational restrictions. It was God's time to make the transition.

After resigning, we received numerous invitations to join other organizations and to pastor various churches, but felt led to decline each one. The Lord impressed on us that we were to wait on Him and not move back into ministry until He directed. We envisaged a few weeks passing, but never imagined it would be as long as eighteen months.

So the waiting period began. With new intensity I sought the Lord for release. Now every day and night I was free to press in to God. No responsibilities. The Lord provided our financial needs until Shirley could obtain a good position which then became our source of income. Our obedience to God in this period of our lives was to bring to birth practical understanding of the unseen world and of how we can release the provisions of Calvary.

Hour by hour I walked the country roads praying. Our house was on the edge of a small town in the midst of beautiful countryside. My only companion was a sheep dog who faithfully followed me wherever I went. With new intensity I fasted, hoping for the breakthrough. For years and years I had put the responsibility on God Himself. I had said, "Lord, You can do it. You are a miracle-working God. Nothing is impossible to You. Please set me free." My continuous, monotonous pleading could be summed up in one word: HELP!

In the ensuing months I was to learn that if I were to become free, I had to take the responsibility myself, and not put it on God. This was a major lesson. Likewise, I was to learn to stop asking God for His provisions and to receive them by faith. Most of my prayers had been asking, asking, asking, but never receiving.

The first twelve months of waiting passed. Though they were not without numerous blessings, I came to a place where I was exhausted physically, mentally, and spiritually. Every night I was plagued with fearful dreams, waking each morning discouraged and depleted of strength. I had fasted three months of the twelve and had lost physical

9

resistance. Time and time again I had said to the Lord, "Your Word says if we seek You with the whole heart, we will find You. What is the whole heart? How can I possibly seek You more intensely?" I was still to learn that we please God by faith; not by religious exercises such as fasting and praying, important as they are.

Looking back, we can see what the Lord was permitting: He was bringing us to a place of death before resurrection. We had served Him faithfully and zealously, but so much of our labors had been in our own strength. We were going to have to die before we could live.

One day I said to Shirley, "I feel that I am a dead man. I have died to this world. I have died to myself. I have died to serving God. I will never preach again unless there is a miracle. I feel as if I am under the ground and buried. I'm alive and yet I'm dead. I've come to the end of myself."

For some time I felt this way. But in the midst of the darkness, when it seemed I could go no lower, the Lord began to teach me how I could rise in resurrection life.

What He taught is what we share with you in the following chapters.

Chapter 2

Shirley's Testimony

"I feel that I'm a dead man," my husband said to me as he lay on the bed in our spare room. The memory of that occasion is still very real. "I'll never preach again unless God does a miracle." There was nothing I could say. I had no answer that he didn't know, no reason for the seemingly closed heavens, which we hadn't already discussed. But deep in my heart I knew our loving Father knew and cared. He was there in that room of despair, although we couldn't feel Him. I had been born into a wonderful Christian home (a story in itself), and now the truths I had been taught as a child were anchors which kept me. I knew God loved and cared amidst it all, and that He knew what He was doing with us.

When I first met Graham, the thing that attracted me to him was his seeking after God. In my heart I had longed for a partner whose main desire was to know God and do His will. This I found in Graham. It wasn't until after we were married, that I began to understand a little of the inner conflict he was going through.

Our backgrounds were vastly different. He was one of two children: I was one of eleven. The day we married, I went from one extreme to another — from living in a large house with much activity, to a small apartment with one, quiet, young man who had such inner pressures and torment that he was forced to spend much time seeking God. Even when he was with me, he often could not communicate because he was so preoccupied with the battles within himself. "One day I'll be different," he would say to me during the many days of depression. We were always looking to the future, to the day when God would perform a miracle. But the wait went on endlessly.

We were as keen for God as we knew how, seeking and serving Him. Yet as the years went by, our lives became more and more restricted. It seemed the more God worked in us, the more the pressures increased in Graham. He couldn't stand me using hairspray

11

or any kind of perfume because he was allergic to them. He was also allergic to any kind of artificial heating in the house. Any change in temperature immediately started him sneezing. Because of his inward pressures, we often wouldn't accept an invitation to go out; he didn't know if he could handle it or not. His feelings were so unpredictable that he only knew how he would be that day — or that hour. The pressures within him dominated our lives for years. I seemed to be always making excuses for him, often going to church alone or having to cancel an engagement we had made. The torment within him was such that he needed to pray. Nothing else brought any release and even this was only temporary. I was always covering up for him.

Although many times he sought counsel, no one could help him. No one could understand. Even I could not understand his pressures. He seemed to be alone in his sufferings.

Then God began to show him the way of faith. I remember the day he grasped the truth of faith and of our rights as children of God. It came as a revelation to him. This was a new day for us — a day of hope. From then on, he began to gradually change.

Having grasped the truths, nothing could stop him. Warfare was a priority every day. The inner release became more and more evident. The depressions went. His personality stabilized. I saw him change from a shy, introverted young man, to one of confidence and authority in God. A change that not only altered his personality, but also his appearance. A change so obvious that others expressed their amazement. A change which only took place as he put into practice what he has shared in the pages of this book.

It wasn't until Graham began changing, that I realized I needed deliverance too. Me? with a background so wonderful and protected, needed deliverance! It was hard to believe, and yet it became more and more evident. I was finding it difficult to keep adjusting to a new man. He was gradually becoming more and more confident. No longer did I have to make excuses for him or shield him. We began to live a normal life. He was becoming more independent; able to stand for himself; able to meet commitments. Through this time, I began to see many holds of the enemy in my own life.

Rejection was one area where, after deliverance, I changed dramatically. Graham was now praying for others, and the results were such that he was kept busy with many coming for counsel. I was often left alone. Many nights he would be late coming home. At any time he could be called upon to pray for someone. My reactions were such that he discerned holds of rejection, frustration, and loneliness that had come from childhood. Although my background had been all I could have wished for, being one of eleven children didn't allow the time a child needs with its parents. Although I was loved and wanted, a stronghold of rejection developed in my life, and now it was causing me to be unable to cope with my new husband.

And so I too began on my road to freedom. The change was wonderful. I had often wanted to be different — to react differently. After deliverance, the unwanted reactions were no longer within me. Graham's counseling continued. The demands on his time increased. But now I could cope with and enjoy my new husband. There was a wonderful peace within.

Another stronghold in my life was sorrow. It started when an elder brother died while I was forming in the womb. The sorrow of the occasion affected me. It manifested when I was separated from those I loved. During my childhood and teenage years, other separations happened that strengthened the hold until a separation was something I dreaded. I recognized this stronghold when God was moving us once again to a new location and our farewell was scheduled. The thought of it was so traumatic that I knew something was wrong. I discerned "sorrow through separation." (By this time I was recognizing my own needs and praying myself through.) After coming against it and binding its power over my emotions, I knew release had come. I faced the separation with a strength that proved I was free. Separations were no longer the trauma they had been. How grateful I was to God.

Infirmity was another area in which I saw wonderful changes. Many more illustrations could be added of different areas in my life that have been dealt with. The message we bring you has transformed us enabling us to live normal lives. We count it a privilege to share with you, and pray that Jesus Christ Himself will be revealed to you as The Deliverer.

Chapter 3

The Greatness of God

In the coming chapters considerable attention will be focused on Satan and his works. As we see the extent of his power and effect on mankind, we must be careful not to find ourselves standing in awe of his apparent greatness and might.

It is true that Satan is powerful. He is the god of this world, and for this reason I don't joke about him or refer to him by casual names such as "the old devil." His power, however, when compared with God's power, is as nothing. If we only look at Satan, then Satan is very great; but if we look at him in comparison to God, then he is very small.

In my own experience while struggling against the powers of darkness which at times were extremely strong, it was always a great comfort to know that the God to whom I constantly looked, was a God of all-might and supreme power — far, far greater than Satan who was merely a created being and one whose power had been broken by a triumphant Christ!

One day Psalm 113 was quickened to me by the Holy Spirit:

Verse 4: *The Lord is high above all nations; His glory is above the heavens.*

I recalled Solomon pondering while he considered the building of an earthly temple for the name of the Lord. He said, *"But who is able to build a house for Him, for the heavens and the highest heavens cannot contain Him?"* . . . *(2 Chronicles 2:6).* Again, after the temple was built, he declared, *"But will God indeed dwell with mankind on the earth? Behold, heaven and the highest heaven [literally "heaven of heavens"] cannot contain Thee; how much less this house which I have built" (2 Chronicles 6:18).*

Solomon in his understanding did not have a small God, but one who could not be contained even by the heaven of heavens.

Verse 5: *Who is like the Lord our God, Who is enthroned on high?*

This is a rhetorical question, the obvious answer being: "No one is like the Lord our God who is enthroned on high." No one can compare with Him. No one else, including Satan, deserves a mention. Even the greatest creature of God's creation appears as a minute speck of dust in comparison with the Lord who towers in His glory like an almighty mountain. A speck of dust as against a mountain! Is there a comparison? Can the smaller challenge the greater? Can Satan challenge God?

Verse 6 particularly stood out to me: *Who [God] humbles Himself to behold the things that are in heaven and in the earth.*

My heart leapt within me. I was lifted up to sense God's greatness in a new way. Think of it! God has to humble Himself to look at the earth. Not only that, God has to humble Himself to look at the heavens!

My imagination came alive: I saw man, so very, very small. Man standing upon an earth that seemed large to him, yet from God's viewpoint so minute. Man reaching out into the starry heavens with powerful telescopes, searching the vast expanses of the universe. Light traveling at 186,000 miles per second. Universes millions and millions of light years away. Man unable to find their end, but God seeing and knowing them all. And then to think that there was coming a day when the universe would be cast aside as a mantle (Hebrews 1:11-12), and God would create new heavens and a new earth (2 Peter 3:10-13).

I envisaged a Mighty, Omnipotent God holding, not man in His hand, not the earth, but the entire universe. He holds it in His hand as a grain of sand. From God's point of view, the universe is so small that He has to humble Himself even to look at it; let alone to consider the tiny planet called Earth; still less to consider a tiny creature called man.

Let us see the Lord for who He is: the Creator, the Source of all life, the Sustainer of all things, the Almighty God! Then let us realize the smallness of Satan. Our enemy tries to reverse the picture: to cause us to see himself as the mighty one and God as the small one. Let us not be deceived.

It is also important to keep in mind that Almighty God has exalted His Son, Jesus Christ, and given Him the position of highest authority in the universe. Ephesians 1:20-21 says that God . . . *seated Him [Jesus] at His right hand in the heavenly places, far above all*

16

rule and authority and power and dominion, and every name that is named, not only in this age, but also in the one to come.

As Christians we serve the Almighty, all-powerful God. As we go forward in the name of Jesus Christ, the name which is above every other name, there is no need whatever for us to fear a confrontation with the kingdom of darkness.

Chapter 4

The Mystery of Satan

It was a busy Saturday night on the streets of Wellington, New Zealand. As was my custom, I was out preaching the gospel. This night the crowd was particularly boisterous.

A woman interjector was actively at work. Contradicting what I was saying, she called out, "We are all God's children! Everyone is a child of God!"

Quickly I responded, "No! That's not right! We are all in one of two families: either the family of God, or the family of Satan." And to prove my point, I began quoting Scriptures about the kingdom of God and the kingdom of Satan.

Suddenly there was another interjection: "Here I am!! Here I am!!"

I looked up and for a moment was speechless. Before me stood "the devil himself" — a man on his way to a fancy-dress party. He had on a red costume with pointed ears; his face was blackened and he was brandishing a trident. The crowd turned and laughed. Gathering myself together, I began to share from the Bible the true description of Satan and of his defeat by Jesus Christ.

Among both Christians and non-Christians, there are many false ideas about Satan and his kingdom. Some even think that Satan is not a real person. They see him merely as a figment of the imagination — man's imaginary personification of the source of evil.

Others accept that Satan and evil spirits are real, but having little understanding of this unseen realm, are afraid of them. The realm is "spooky"; mysterious; something they would rather stay away from. Some Christians are afraid of reprisal should they "upset" the devil.

These concepts and fears are contrary to Scripture. It is Satan and his hosts who are afraid of us. They know that we, as believers in Christ, rightfully have authority over them. Satan is very clever; and if he can cause people to believe he doesn't exist, or cause them to make a mockery of his reality, then he has gained a great advantage. His aim is to keep us in ignorance both about himself and about our position and authority in Christ.

If we are going to win a battle, we must know the enemy. We must not allow ourselves to remain in ignorance, but must acquaint ourselves with what the Scriptures teach. Then, as Paul told the Corinthians, Satan will have no advantage over us, for we will not be ignorant of his schemes (2 Corinthians 2:11).

There are two Old Testament passages which give significant insight into the origin and fall of Satan: Isaiah 14 and Ezekiel 28. In these passages, Isaiah speaks of the king of Babylon and Ezekiel of the king of Tyre. Their words, however, go beyond these kings to describe Satan himself. This can be likened to the messianic Psalms where David, apparently making reference to himself, was actually describing Christ (e.g. Psalm 22).

ISAIAH 14:

12 *"How you have fallen from heaven,*
O star of the morning [AV: Lucifer], son of the dawn!
You have been cut down to the earth,
You who have weakened the nations!

13 *"But you said in your heart,*
'I will ascend to heaven;
I will raise my throne above the stars of God,
And I will sit on the mount of assembly
In the recesses of the north.

14 *'I will ascend above the heights of the clouds;*
I will make myself like the Most High.'

15 *"Nevertheless you will be thrust down to Sheol,*
To the recesses of the pit."

EZEKIEL 28

12 *"Son of man, take up a lamentation over the king of Tyre, and say*
to him, 'Thus says the Lord God,
"You had the seal of perfection,
Full of wisdom and perfect in beauty.

13 *"You were in Eden, the garden of God;*
Every precious stone was your covering:
The ruby, the topaz, and the diamond;
The beryl, the onyx, and the jasper;
The lapis lazuli, the turquoise, and the emerald;
And the gold, the workmanship of your settings [or
"tambourines"] and sockets [or "flutes"],

Was in you.
On the day that you were created
They were prepared.
14 *"You were the anointed cherub who covers,*
And I placed you there.
You were on the holy mountain of God;
You walked in the midst of the stones of fire.
15 *"You were blameless in your ways*
From the day you were created,
Until unrighteousness was found in you.
16 *"By the abundance of your trade*
You were internally filled with violence,
And you sinned;
Therefore I have cast you as profane
From the mountain of God.
And I have destroyed you, O covering cherub,
From the midst of the stones of fire.
17 *"Your heart was lifted up because of your beauty;*
You corrupted your wisdom by reason of your splendor.
I cast you to the ground;
I put you before kings,
That they may see you." ' "

1. The Origin of Satan

God is the only One who has always existed. He was never created, but has existed from all eternity.

God created all other spiritual beings. This includes the angels, the cherubim, the seraphim (Genesis 3:24; Isaiah 6:1-7; Revelation 4:6-9), and also Satan (Ezekiel 28:13, 15). It is important to remember this: Satan, like us, is only a created being. How much smaller is the creation than the Creator!

Satan, when created, was not evil. We are told he "had the seal of perfection" and was "full of wisdom and perfect in beauty" (Ezekiel 28:12). His name originally was Lucifer meaning "bright and shining one" (Isaiah 14:12 AV). God created a beautiful Lucifer, perfect in all his ways. He appears to have been one of the greatest, if not the greatest, of the angelic beings. He was the "anointed cherub who covers" (Ezekiel 28:14). This meant he would have been responsible for guarding the throne of God. There is also indication that he was a master musician (Ezekiel 28:13; Isaiah 14:11).

2. The Fall of Satan

Lucifer, lifted up by pride in his God-given beauty and wisdom, chose to rebel against his Maker and be like God. In his self-will he rebelled against God's will. He chose to be independent of God. Isaiah 14:13-14 speaks of five "I wills" of Lucifer's ambition:

I will ascend to heaven.

I will raise my throne above the stars of God.

I will sit on the mount of assembly.

I will ascend above the heights of the clouds.

I will make myself like the Most High.

His lawlessness brought the retribution of God upon him, and he was cast . . . *as profane from the mountain of God* . . . (Ezekiel 28:16).

Jesus said in Luke 10:18: *"I was watching Satan fall from heaven like lightning."*

Revelation 12:9 says: *And the great dragon was thrown down, the serpent of old who is called the devil and Satan, who deceives the whole world; he was thrown down to the earth, and his angels were thrown down with him.*

3. The Hosts of Satan

Lucifer was not alone in his rebellion against the Almighty. He influenced other angels to join him. Just as he was cast down from heaven, so too were they. Many Bible teachers believe that a third of the angelic host was involved:

And his [the great red dragon's] tail swept away a third of the stars of heaven, and threw them to the earth. . . . — Revelation 12:4

Some of these angels are already in a place of confinement awaiting the Day of Judgment, but others are much at work and are yet to be confined.

And angels who did not keep their own domain, but abandoned their proper abode, He has kept in eternal bonds under darkness for the judgment of the great day.   *— Jude 6*

Satan has organized those involved with him into a highly organized confederacy of spirit beings, fulfilling differing functions in differing spheres, and exercising varying degrees of authority and power. Ephesians 6:12 mentions four designations: *For our struggle is not against flesh and blood, but against the rulers, against the powers, against the world forces of this darkness, against the spiritual forces of wickedness in the heavenly places.*

Daniel 10 relates a period in Daniel's life when he had been fasting and praying for three weeks. While he sat on the bank of the Tigris River, an angel appeared to him and said, . . . *"Do not be afraid, Daniel, for from the first day that you set your heart on understanding this and on humbling yourself before your God, your words were heard, and I have come in response to your words" (verse 12).*

The angel was sent from God's presence on the first day of Daniel's fast, but was delayed in his coming by spiritual powers in the heavenlies. *"But the prince of the kingdom of Persia was withstanding me for twenty-one days; then behold, Michael, one of the chief princes, came to help me, for I had been left there with the kings of Persia" (verse 13).*

The prince of the kingdom of Persia and the kings of Persia who withstood the angel were not the human, earthly potentates, but angelic rulers who held an unseen, domineering influence over the Persian Empire.

While we clearly recognize separate nations with their human governments, we may not always appreciate that in the unseen realm there are corresponding angelic rulers who influence the human spheres and endeavor to enforce the dictates of their satanic head.

Satan's confederacy could be likened to the armed forces of a nation headed by a commander in chief under whom are generals, colonels, majors, and so on, right down to the lowest rank, the private.

As Christians, we are involved in a spiritual war against these unseen wicked powers.

4. The Domain of Satan

Satan's activities are now confined to the "heavenly places" which include the atmosphere of planet earth on which we live. This is a lower sphere than his first estate at the Throne of God.

When Jesus ascended, He . . . *passed through the heavens . . . (Hebrews 4:14),* and . . . *ascended far above all the heavens . . . (Ephesians 4:10).*

Satan has special influence and activities on planet earth. In Ephesians 2:2 he is called "the prince of the power of the air," and in 2 Corinthians 4:4 "the god of this world." Jesus referred to Satan as "the ruler of the world" (John 14:30).

When Satan tempted the Lord Jesus, he spoke assuming that all the kingdoms of the world were his, and in the final temptation offered them to Jesus (Matthew 4:8-9). In reply Jesus did not dispute Satan's jurisdiction over them.

When John wrote Revelation, Satan's earthly headquarters were situated at or near Pergamum (Revelation 2:12-13), and perhaps are still there today. Pergamum was located in the country we now call Turkey, a nation that today restricts the preaching of the gospel and has an extremely small Christian population. Interesting!

5. The Names of Satan

Before his fall, he was called **Lucifer, son of the morning** (Isaiah 14:12 AV) — terms that describe his brightness and shining appearance. Ezekiel 28:14 calls him the **anointed cherub**.

Since his fall, the following names apply: They are names that clearly highlight his depravity and evil purposes.

Satan — Adversary (one who is hostile, opposing, against). Matthew 4:10; Zechariah 3:1

Devil — Accuser, slanderer. Matthew 4:1; John 8:44

Serpent — A snake. Genesis 3:1; Revelation 12:9

Dragon — Revelation 12:3-17

Abaddon or Apollyon — Destroyer. Revelation 9:11

Belial — Worthless, perverse. 2 Corinthians 6:15

Beelzebul — "Lord of the flies" — a dung god of the Ekronites. Matthew 12:24, 27

Enemy — Matthew 13:39

Adversary — 1 Peter 5:8

Oppressor — One who has dominion over. Acts 10:38

Accuser — Revelation 12:10

Murderer — Destroyer of life. John 8:44

Liar — John 8:44

Angel of Light — 2 Corinthians 11:14

Roaring Lion — 1 Peter 5:8

Deceiver — Revelation 12:9; 2 Corinthians 11:3

Prince of the power of the air — Ephesians 2:2

God of this world — 2 Corinthians 4:4

Ruler of the world — John 12:31; 14:30; 16:11

Ruler of the demons — Matthew 12:24

Tempter — Matthew 4:3

Wolf — John 10:12

Thief — John 10:10

Antichrist — 1 John 4:1-4; 2 John 7

Angel of the Abyss — Revelation 9:11
Condemner — 1 Timothy 3:6
Evil One — Matthew 13:19
King — Revelation 9:11
Trapper — Psalm 91:3

6. The Hostility of Satan

Satan opposes God and all that God's kingdom stands for.

In the beginning of human history, when Adam and Eve yielded to Satan's temptation and sinned against God, God told Satan there would be One born through Eve's descendants who would rise and overcome him:

And I will put enmity
Between you and the woman,
And between your seed and her seed;
He shall bruise you on the head,
And you shall bruise him on the heel. — Genesis 3:15

How Satan tried to hinder the fulfillment of this word! When Jesus was born, Satan, knowing He was the One that God had said would come, set about to do all he could to destroy Him.

Through Herod, he unleashed his fury, ordering the murder of all male children two years old and under in and around Bethlehem, hoping to kill Jesus in the process. But an angel prewarned Joseph and he fled with his family to Egypt (Matthew 2).

Another attempt was made on His life soon after He was baptized in the Holy Spirit and had commenced His ministry. This time, through the hostility of people in His home town, Satan tried to have Him thrown over a cliff; but he was unsuccessful (Luke 4:16-30).

Not accepting defeat, Satan sought access to Jesus through those who were closest to Him. In Judas, one of the twelve, he found a place. But the Lord knew of Satan's scheming and what the final outcome would be (John 6:70-71; Luke 18:31-33).

In his desperation to destroy the Son of God, Satan entered into Judas who betrayed Jesus (John 13:21-30). Then, stirring the crowds to hostility with their cries of "Crucify Him!", Satan, through Pilate, committed Jesus to the shameful death of crucifixion. With Jesus nailed to the cross, Satan thought he had triumphed. But by the wisdom of God, what Satan saw as his triumph, turned out to be his utter and complete defeat.

But we speak God's wisdom in a mystery, the hidden wisdom, which God predestined before the ages to our glory; the wisdom which none of the rulers of this age has understood; for if they had understood it, they would not have crucified the Lord of glory.

— I Corinthians 2:7-8

After the resurrection, Satan, although defeated, still did not give in. His hostility turned to the disciples as they went out to preach and teach in Jesus' name. Tradition tells us that all but one of the twelve apostles died as martyrs.

Over the centuries this hostility has continued against the body of true believers; but even to this day, the enemy has not been able to wipe out those who bear testimony to the reality that Jesus Christ is Lord.

Jesus said . . . *"I will build My church; and the gates of Hades shall not overpower it"* (Matthew 16:18).

7. The Limitations of Satan

Limited in Power

Although Satan wields much power and influence over humanity, it is Almighty God who has the final say and is sovereign in human affairs. Satan can only go as far as God allows him. We see this clearly in the story of Job.

Initially, Satan had not been able to touch Job because God had made a hedge around him and his house and all that he had (Job 1:10). Then at Satan's request, God gave him permission to touch his possessions, but not Job himself. With this permission, Satan destroyed Job's donkeys, oxen, sheep, camels, servants, and sons and daughters; but Job was unharmed (Job 1:11-19). Next God gave Satan permission to touch Job's bones and flesh, but not his life. Again Satan acted only within the limits of the permission granted him, and he afflicted Job with boils, but he could not take his life (Job 2:4-7). It was God who had the final say.

Luke 22:31-32 is another interesting passage: *"Simon, Simon, behold, Satan has demanded permission to sift you like wheat; but I have prayed for you, that your faith may not fail."* . . . Here we see Satan wanting to work against Peter; but without permission, he couldn't do it. Permission was granted, but Jesus prayed that Peter's faith would not fail. Satan could only do to Peter what the Lord allowed.

Limited in Time

   . . . Woe to the earth and the sea, because the devil has come down to you, having great wrath, knowing that he has only a short time.
                                                          — Revelation 12:12

   God has set a day when final judgment will be executed and the righteous will be free forever from satanic influence.

   Satan is aware of this, and so also are evil spirits. On one occasion when Jesus was casting evil spirits out of a man, they cried out, *"What do we have to do with You, Son of God? Have You come here to torment us before the time?" (Matthew 8:29).*

Limited in Location

   God is omnipresent, that is, He is everywhere all the time. In contrast, Satan, like us, is limited to one geographical location at any one time. Job 1:6-7. It is only with the aid of other fallen spirit beings that he is able to operate simultaneously all over the world.

8. The Worship of Satan

   In desiring to make himself like the Most High (Isaiah 14:14), Satan was not only wanting to exercise dominion over God's creation, but longing for the worship of His created beings.

   Satan even sought worship from Jesus. He desired it so much that he was willing to offer Jesus all the kingdoms of the world and their glory if He would only fall down and worship him (Matthew 4:8-9).

   From very early times, Satan has been luring mankind into worshipping himself. By drawing men's hearts and minds away from the living God, the deceiver finds great satisfaction. Romans 1:25 tells us that mankind exchanged the truth of God for the lie of Satan, and began worshipping and serving the creature rather than the Creator. From the glory of God, they turned to images of men and animals (verse 23).

   By fashioning idols of human likeness or other forms and then bowing and worshipping them, man is worshipping demons.

   What do I mean then? That a thing sacrificed to idols is anything, or that an idol is anything? No, but I say that the things which the Gentiles sacrifice, they sacrifice to demons, and not to God; and I do not want you to become sharers in demons. You cannot drink the cup of the Lord and the cup of demons; you cannot partake of the table of the Lord and the table of demons.   *— I Corinthians 10:19-21*

And the rest of mankind, who were not killed by these plagues, did not repent of the works of their hands, so as not to worship demons, and the idols of gold and of silver and of brass and of stone and of wood, which can neither see nor hear nor walk.

— Revelation 9:20

In worshipping demons, man is paying homage to Satan, the ruler of the demons. Even to this day, millions of the earth's population worship Satan through bowing before idols. Because they are deceived, many do not know that this is what they are actually doing.

You may think that idolatry has no part in your life. But take care. The Bible extends the scope of idolatry to include idols within our imaginations that we covet or lust after. Colossians 3:5 says: *Therefore consider the members of your earthly body as dead to immorality, impurity, passion, evil desire, and greed, which amounts to idolatry.* Let us check that there are no idols of this kind that draw our fascination, our time, our energy, and our worship.

Satan is strategically working towards the day when, through the antichrist, he will achieve his full lust for worship.

And all who dwell on the earth will worship him, everyone whose name has not been written from the foundation of the world in the book of life of the Lamb who has been slain. — *Revelation 13:8*

9. The Defeat of Satan

When Jesus died, Satan thought he had won a great victory. Instead the opposite was true.

Since then the children share in flesh and blood, He Himself likewise also partook of the same, that through death He might render powerless him who had the power of death, that is, the devil; and might deliver those who through fear of death were subject to slavery all their lives. — *Hebrews 2:14-15*

. . . I was dead, and behold, I am alive forevermore, and I have the keys of death and of Hades. — *Revelation 1:18*

Raised from the lowest hell by the Father, Jesus triumphed over satanic rulers and authorities, and made a public display of them. Colossians 2:15.

The victory that Jesus Christ won was not for Himself, but for us (Hebrews 2:15). Jesus has always been the eternal Son of God, the One by whose Word creation came into being (John 1:1-3). Coming from heaven, He divested Himself of His eternal glory and power, and walked this earth as a man. As the Son of Man, anointed by the Holy

28

Spirit, He overcame Satan for us. We, as fallen humanity, were under satanic slavery — slavery to sin (Romans 6:17-18).

Jesus became sin for us . . . *that we might become the right-eousness of God in Him (2 Corinthians 5:21).* He offered Himself as a substitutionary sacrifice at the cross. Being a sinless offering, and being a perfect man, He bore the judgment due to mankind through the breaking of God's law. Divine justice was appeased through this once-for-all sacrifice, making it legally possible for God to receive the repentant sinner, not on the basis of his righteousness, but because of the blood of the Lord Jesus (Matthew 26:28). Thus the sinner is freed from Satan's power.

Our freedom from Satan's power, however, only becomes effective in our lives when we individually come to Jesus Christ by faith, confessing our sins and turning from our own way, and yielding to Him as Lord. Only then does His victory over Satan become our victory. Apart from the Lord Jesus, we have no power to rise above satanic influence. Acts 4:12; Revelation 12:11.

10. The Destiny of Satan

Satan and his angels will never be reconciled to God. Their eternal future is clearly defined in the Word of God: *And the devil who deceived them was thrown into the lake of fire and brimstone, where the beast and the false prophet are also; and they will be tormented day and night forever and ever (Revelation 20:10).*

Sharing this same destiny will be all of humanity who fail to repent and turn to Jesus Christ as Lord and Savior. In Matthew 25 Jesus talked of His ultimate return to this earth and of the gathering of the nations before Him for judgment (verses 31-32). To those who had failed to honor and obey Him, He said, . . . *"Depart from Me, accursed ones, into the eternal fire which has been prepared for the devil and his angels" (verse 41).* In verse 46, He describes the eternal fire as "eternal punishment."

As you read this book, let the awareness of Satan's eternal defeat be before you. Judgment Day is coming; sin will be accounted for; and Satan will be assigned to eternal retribution.

Chapter 5

The Realm of Demons

Because Satan is limited to one location at any one time, he has to use his evil agents to carry out his purposes. As mentioned in Chapter 4, Satan and his agents are well organized with varying ranks and varying degrees of responsibility. Demons comprise the lower orders and cause the bondages in human lives. We seldom deal directly with Satan; rather, we deal with him indirectly through evil spirits.

The terms "demons" and "evil spirits" are synonymous and are being used interchangeably.

1. The Origin of Demons

Scripture does not tell us the origin of demons. However, various speculations have been put forward. For example: fallen angels; disembodied spirits from a pre-Adamic creation; and spirits of the unnatural offspring of angels and human women prior to the flood in the days of Noah.

I do not lean to any theory as to their origin, excepting that I do not believe they are fallen angels. Acts 23:8-9 makes a distinction between spirits and angels.

We may speculate as to the origin of demons, but if the Scripture is silent, it is not necessary for us to know. What we do know is that demons are real and we have been given the means to be victorious over them.

2. The Personality of Demons

Demons are living, intelligent beings. They are not merely indistinct forces affecting human lives. Their personalities are totally corrupt, bearing the likeness of Satan, and fulfilling his wicked purposes. They want to spoil the divine likeness of man made in the image of God.

It seems, however, that they are disembodied. They have their own personalities, but no body in which to live. They crave, therefore, to indwell human beings in order to be able to express their personalities more fully.

They display personality characteristics: will, knowledge, emotion, speech, and self-awareness.

(a) Will

Now when the unclean spirit goes out of a man, it passes through waterless places, seeking rest, and does not find it. Then it says, "I will return to my house from which I came." . . .
— *Matthew 12:43-44*

Demons make decisions. They can choose. "I will return to my house." Many times in counseling sessions, I have heard demons cry out through people's lips defying the commands to go with cries such as, "I will not go! I will never go!"

(b) Knowledge

And just then there was in their synagogue a man with an unclean spirit; and he cried out, saying, "What do we have to do with You, Jesus of Nazareth? Have You come to destroy us? I know who You are — the Holy One of God!" — *Mark 1:23-24*

Although the world of man was slow to know the identify of Jesus, the Son of God, the unseen spirit world knew. "I know who You are — the Holy One of God!" Evil spirits have knowledge. We see this also in Acts 19:15:

And the evil spirit answered and said to them, "I recognize Jesus, and I know about Paul, but who are you?"

(c) Emotion

You believe that God is one. You do well; the demons also believe, and shudder. — *James 2:19*

The word *shudder* in Greek means "to bristle, to shiver, to have the hair on end." Demons express much emotion, whether the person indwelt by them feels it or not.

When Philip went to Samaria and preached Christ to the people, we read: *For in the case of many who had unclean spirits, they were coming out of them shouting with a loud voice; and many who had been paralyzed and lame were healed" (Acts 8:7).* "Loud voice" indicates emotion.

In deliverance meetings I have held, all sorts of manifestations have been experienced. One could never doubt that demons express emotion. They are afraid of believers exercising their authority in Christ.

(d) Speech

And whenever the unclean spirits beheld Him, they would fall down before Him and cry out, saying, "You are the Son of God!" And He earnestly warned them not to make Him known. — *Mark 3:11-12*

In this passage the demons clearly and loudly spoke to Jesus who then commanded them not to make Him known. Demons often speak through people, especially during times of deliverance.

One day when I was praying for someone in a deliverance service, a demon vented its hatred at me and spoke harshly through a normally quiet and gentle person: "I hate you! I hate you and all that you stand for!" These were strange words to be coming from some-one who was a good friend and with whom we enjoyed a good relationship. Obviously the words were not coming from the person, but from the demon.

When this happened, it highlighted the source behind opposition and bitterness that Shirley and I were at that time encountering from a small group of people in the church because we had disciplined one of their number for continuing in a sin that was affecting harmony in our music team. The words of the demon confirmed that it was not so much the people who were speaking against us (although they were willfully involved), but that there was flak coming through them from a demonic source.

(e) Self-Awareness

And crying out with a loud voice, he said, "What do I have to do with You, Jesus, Son of the Most High God? I implore You by God, do not torment me!" For He had been saying to him, "Come out of the man, you unclean spirit!" And He was asking him, "What is your name?" And he said to Him, "My name is Legion; for we are many."
— *Mark 5:7-9*

When Jesus asked the spirit its name, it replied, "My name is Legion; for we are many." The spirit was aware of itself and knew its name. Every spirit has a name and knows its function.

33

3. Possession by Demons

Demons look upon the human body as their home:

Now when the unclean spirit goes out of a man, it passes through waterless places, seeking rest, and does not find it. Then it says, "I will return to my house from which I came"; and when it comes, it finds it unoccupied, swept, and put in order. Then it goes, and takes along with it seven other spirits more wicked than itself, and they go in and live there. . . . — Matthew 12:43-45

They are extremely reluctant to leave their home, and will usually not go unless they are forcefully evicted. When commanded to leave, spirits often say things such as, "This is my house." "I don't want to go." "I've been here for thirty years and I'm not going."

Evil spirits can also dwell in animals. In Mark 5:1-13 when Jesus was casting a legion of evil spirits out of the Gerasene demoniac, the spirits begged Jesus to send them into a nearby herd of two thousand swine. Jesus gave them permission, and when they entered the swine, the herd immediately ran down a steep bank into the sea and were drowned.

When the enemy's work in my own life was first revealed and I was having sessions of prayer, a dog across the street howled in the most strange manner every time spirits in me began to stir. This went on so consistently that I was certain the dog was demonized. It was always kept penned in the rear yard of the house, but one day it got free. The first thing it did was race next door to a little girl playing on the lawn, and began to maul the helpless child's face. Amid screams, the mother rushed to her aid. The dog had to be destroyed. My suspicion that it was demonized had been confirmed in a most unfortunate way.

Many Christians misunderstand what is meant when it is said that a person has evil spirits. The expression "demon-possessed" is partly to blame. Some versions of the Bible have extensively translated the Greek word *daimonizomai* as "demon-possessed." Unfortunately it carries connotations that suggest the person was completely "filled up" with demons. This has caused many Christians to react against the idea of believers being bound by evil spirits. "How can I be indwelt by the Holy Spirit and yet be possessed by demons?"

A more literal translation of the word *daimonizomai* is "demonized." A demonized person is not necessarily completely controlled by evil spirits. Matthew 9:32 tells of a dumb man, demon-possessed, who was brought to Jesus. Although he had a demon that made him dumb, he was not totally possessed. His body was probably healthy, and his mind clear, although he was unable to express his thoughts because his tongue was tied. After Jesus cast the demon out of that area, he was free to express himself.

Demonization usually occurs only in certain areas of a person's life. A person's body may be well, while his soul is gripped with great depression. His body is not directly under the power of the enemy, but one area of his personality is. A person may experience great peace, and yet have a fear of dogs. Whenever a dog comes his way, he is gripped with fear. The enemy has gained a measure of dominion in his life. He is not possessed in the sense that he is brimming over with nothing but demons; but there is an area which is not under his control. He is demonized in that area.

We will lose the fear of being demon-possessed, if we can understand that in some areas of our lives we can be demonized (that is, under the influence or domination of evil spirits), while in other areas we can be experiencing great liberty.

The Bible uses different terms in regard to possession by demons: to *have* a spirit (Matthew 11:18); to be *with* a spirit (Mark 1:23); to be *demonized* (Luke 8:36); to be *oppressed* (Acts 10:38). "Oppressed" is a translation of the Greek work *katadunasteuo* which means "to exercise power over."

Some people try to differentiate between those who are "demon-possessed," those who are "demon-oppressed," those who are "demon-obsessed," and so on. These classifications are confusing and unnecessarily make simple things complicated. Evil spirits are either on the *inside* or the *outside*. If on the inside, they are to be *cast out*. If on the outside, they are to be *kept out*. I Peter 5:8-9.

4. The Extent of Demonism

The extent of demonism goes far beyond what most Christians — and even Christian leaders — have ever imagined.

In regard to non-Christians, the Bible says: . . . *The god of this world has blinded the minds of the unbelieving, that they might not see the light of the gospel . . . (2 Corinthians 4:4).* Satan blinds the minds of the unbelieving through an inward operation. 2 Corinthians 3:13-16 speaks of a veil upon the minds of unbelievers that is taken away only through turning to Christ.

When the Lord appeared to Paul on the Damascus road and

called him into service, He told Paul he was to go to the Gentiles *to open their eyes so that they may turn from darkness to light and from the dominion of Satan to God . . . (Acts 26:18).*

In writing to the Ephesians, Paul, speaking of the state of the believers before they turned to Christ, says: *And you were dead in your trespasses and sins, in which you formerly walked according to the course of this world, according to the prince of the power of the air, of the spirit that is now working in the sons of disobedience (Ephesians 2:1-2).*

In regard to Christians, I believe that at this time in the history of the church few believers are completely free of all demonic bondage. No doubt many readers will be amazed at this statement and some will find it difficult to accept.

I am not saying that most Christians are problem centered or without great measures of victory and joy. I believe, however, that God sees a need for further release and cleansing within many Christians — even many who are being greatly used by God and who are experiencing powerful anointings of the Holy Spirit. Many dear saints bravely press on in their Christian walk and service, expressing outwardly every evidence of victory, although within they are desperate for answers for personal needs. Others continually suppress memories of past negative experiences, believing that to have victory they have to forget the past, not face it. God wants us to be able to look back over our lives, even to the most traumatic experiences, and find ourselves free from any pain or reaction to them. This is true victory.

In my own testimony, I have no doubt whatsoever that I was both a Christian and demonized. I had tried every other way to overcome my personal problems; but it was not until I recognized the sources as demonic and dealt with them in scriptural ways, that victory came.

Satan will do all he can to prevent us knowing that we are in any measure demonized. He works in the dark, and he likes his agents to stay hidden. He does not want his works revealed.

In the early years of my Christian life, when I sought help from various ministries, one minister did suggest that my problems could be demonic. A time was arranged to go to his home for prayer. With him was an evangelist from Scotland who was known for his ability to cast out demons. For about thirty minutes they prayed earnestly commanding demons to manifest and come out; but nothing happened. Although open to their ministry, I was unaffected by it. There was not a stirring inside me. Because there were no manifestations, they concluded that I had no demons. Afterwards I chuckled to myself, "Fancy thinking I had demons!" What a victory it was for the enemy! He won simply by lying concealed.

I have met other Christians who have had similar experiences. They have had prayer for deliverance, but because there were no manifestations, it was concluded they did not need deliverance. Months or years later, it was found that they were indeed demonized. The demons had stayed hidden. How we need in the church the gift of discernings of spirits!

We need to get away from the idea that the only people bound by demons are mentally deranged madmen. Unfortunately, for too long we have accepted ourselves with our problems. We excuse ourselves by saying I'm this temperament or that; it's in the family; dad was like it, and so am I. All the time the enemy lies securely hidden.

The Bible warns Christians to give no place to the devil: *Be ye angry, and sin not: let not the sun go down upon your wrath: Neither give place to the devil (Ephesians 4:26-27 AV).*

The word "place" in the Greek is *topos* from which we derive English words such as "topic" and "topography." The word is used of a region, or locality, or a place which a person or thing occupies. The verse, therefore, is saying that Christians can give a place in their lives for the devil to occupy. We are warned not to do it.

In 1 John 5:18-19 we read: *We know that whosoever is born of God sinneth not; but he that is begotten of God keepeth himself, and that wicked one toucheth him not. And we know that we are of God, and the whole world lieth in wickedness (AV).*

The word "touch" in Greek is *haptomai* which means primarily "to fasten to, to cling to, to attach oneself to." If we become careless and yield to the power of sin, we give the enemy a legal right to fasten to us. This is a clear description of how demons work: they fasten to areas. I have been through countless personal deliverances where spirits leaving my life had to be, as it were, pulled off, unclutched — gripping to the end, when suddenly they would have to let go as authority was exercised over them.

When Jesus summoned His disciples, the first thing He did was give them authority over unclean spirits: *And having summoned His twelve disciples, He gave them authority over unclean spirits, to cast them out, and to heal every kind of disease and every kind of sickness (Matthew 10:1).*

Jesus then sent the twelve out and instructed them: . . . *"Do not go in the way of the Gentiles, and do not enter any city of the Samaritans; but rather go to the lost sheep of the house of Israel. And as you go, preach, saying, 'The kingdom of heaven is at hand.' Heal the sick, raise the dead, cleanse the lepers, cast out demons; freely you received, freely give" (Matthew 10:5-8).* Notice that they were not to go to the Gentiles, but to the lost sheep of the house of Israel.

It was not just an occasional person out of whom demons were cast, but many people: *And when evening had come, they brought to Him many who were demon-possessed; and He cast out the spirits with a word, and healed all who were ill (Matthew 8:16).*

After the resurrection when Jesus was commissioning the disciples to preach the gospel in all the world, He said: *"And these signs will accompany those who have believed: in My name they will cast out demons . . ." (Mark 16:17).*

Some say Christians cannot be demon-possessed. If this is the case, then Jesus has commanded us to go to unbelievers and cast out demons. I cannot see that this could be so; and I have not yet met a Christian who felt he had a ministry of casting demons out of unbelievers. True, there are times when receiving deliverance is the means of bringing someone to Christ, but apart from this, there is no point in bringing deliverance to unbelievers. They are mostly not in a place to want it; or to be able to receive it; or if they are delivered, to be able to maintain it. Deliverance is primarily for believers.

In the early church it was so important and necessary for evil spirits to be driven out, that in Mark 16 it was mentioned first in the list of signs to follow those who believe. But what has happened today? Most churches never cast out demons. To a large degree, we have disobeyed the commission of Jesus and we are reaping the results in our church life. Every leader, every believer, should know how to cast out demons. Not all will major on it, but all can and should know how.

By and large we have preached a gospel that is less than the gospel. Many evangelists preach an easy believism: no repentance, no yielding to Christ as Lord, no necessity for water baptism, no casting out of demons, no infilling of the Holy Spirit. Many have been encouraged to come into the kingdom of God under a please-come-to-Jesus call.

Even those who have wholeheartedly come to Jesus have often not been joined to churches with leaders equipped with spiritual understanding to release them from their bondages. That which should have happened at or subsequent to conversion has never happened. God cannot be blamed. His Word is clear. We need to recognize what the enemy has done, and rise up and deal with him.

This a new day. Our heavenly Father wants His children to be clean and free. In the restoration of truth to His church, the truth of deliverance must find its place. As with any truth, there will be some who will reject it; but praise God many have, and many will, welcome new light and come into new liberty.

5. Numbers of Demons

There are a great many spirit beings. In Revelation 5:11 we are given a glimpse of many angels in the vicinity of God's throne: *And I looked, and I heard the voice of many angels around the throne and the living creatures and the elders; and the number of them was myriads of myriads, and thousands of thousands.*

Fallen angels also exist in large numbers, if they comprise one third of the angels. Likewise we can expect that evil spirits exist in very large numbers.

In Revelation 9:1-11 we read of the bottomless pit being opened and out of it coming forth hideous-looking locusts which were in actual fact hosts of satanic beings. Can you imagine how many locusts in a plague large enough to affect all men on earth who do not have the seal of God on their foreheads? This is the number of the satanic beings loosed from the pit.

In Revelation 9:13-16 we read that when the four angels by the Euphrates River were loosed, there came forth an army of horsemen numbering two hundred million. Again, an enormous number.

Evil spirits can live in great numbers in the lives of men and women. In Mark 5 we read the story of the man with an unclean spirit who lived in the country of the Gerasenes. When Jesus asked the spirit its name, it replied, . . . *"My name is legion; for we are many."* A legion was a military unit of the Roman army made up of infantry and supporting cavalry numbering three to six thousand men. Out of this man, Jesus cast thousands of spirits. So many and so influencial were they, that when given leave by Jesus, they entered a nearby herd of two thousand swine and drove them down an embankment to their death in the sea.

I believe the reason why Jesus granted the evil spirits their request to enter the swine was to alleviate the suffering the man would otherwise have had to go through as he was delivered. Evil spirits often manifest violently as they come out. Had thousands of spirits exerted their strength all at once, it would have been devastating for the man. By granting their request, they left somewhat more willingly and less violently, their violence then being taken out on the swine.

Multitudes of people today need deliverance, not from just a few demons, but from many. After the Lord revealed to me how to break down spiritual strongholds, I discovered as time went by that I, a God-fearing minister of the gospel, had to be released from many, many spirits. No wonder I had had problems! No wonder the wisdom of man had been helpless to release me! Spiritual bondages had to be broken with spiritual weapons in spiritual warfare.

6. The Forms of Demons

With natural eyes we perceive natural things: with spiritual eyes we perceive spiritual things. God can open our spiritual eyes so that we begin to see spiritual things — both from God's kingdom and from the kingdom of darkness.

A minister I know, who had been released from migraine headaches, was one night seated in a tent campaign watching an evangelist pray for a person with migraines. As he watched, his eyes were opened to see a green snake wrapped around the person's head. When the migraine was rebuked, the snake left and came straight for him. Immediately he claimed protection in Jesus' name, and it went past. Turning, he saw the snake-like spirit wrap itself around the head of an associate evangelist who had just walked into the rear of the meeting. The whole of the next day, that evangelist suffered a shocking migraine.

It is interesting that he saw the evil spirit in the form of a snake — the same form in which Satan appeared to Eve in the Garden of Eden. There is a close relationship in Scripture between the animal world and the demonic. In Luke 10:19 evil spirits are referred to as serpents and scorpions. Revelation 16:13 speaks of "three unclean spirits like frogs." In Revelation 9:7-11 we read of satanic hosts appearing as hideous-looking locusts with faces like men's faces, hair like women's hair, teeth like lions' teeth, and tails like those of a scorpion.

I was at a deliverance meeting where a young boy saw spirits like frogs and insects hopping and crawling from the meeting. "Where did all those strange creatures come from?" he asked his mother as he tried to leave her to see where they were going. He was not afraid — just curious.

As well as animal forms, demons can have other grotesque and hideous forms. If we look at carved gods on heathen temples we see fearful, gruesome, repulsive demonic representations that millions bow down to and worship.

While praying for a young man, who had unknown to me been involved in yoga before his conversion, I saw a spirit leaving him that had a most hideous form. It could best be compared to an Indian-type god. That evening as I contemplated the incident, I realized that the spirit had been in a sitting-yoga position as it rose from him and disappeared.

When Shirley and I were in Papua New Guinea praying for a missionary, the Lord showed me that a curse of death had been placed upon him. My eyes were opened to see numerous spirits binding him because of the curse. Their faces were horrible and just like the masks the people carve and wear in their demonic rituals. They fled as we came against them in Jesus' name.

In this same country, we visited a school where some time before, a student had begun screaming while walking in the school grounds. A Christian teacher took her to his home, where she related that she had seen an evil spirit that terrified her. Interested, the teacher asked, "What did it look like?" Turning and pointing to a Papua New Guinean mask on the wall, she said, "Like that! It looked just like that!" The convicted teacher hurriedly destroyed his souvenir.

Most of us do not see the form or shape of evil spirits, nor do we have to. It is enough to know that they are vile creatures — vile in appearance, character, and works. Let us give no place to them.

One concern I have is the type of puppets that children see through agencies such as TV. Although many of these puppets look delightful and humorous, there are some that are hideous and frightening, especially to small children. From where comes the inspiration for the fashioning of these puppets? Should we not as parents supervise what our children watch so that they will not open themselves to spirits of fear. We should not over-protect our children, but there is a measure of protection that we must give.

Again, what is the inspiration behind characters such as fairies, elves, gnomes, and witches? These are forms of demons. I have known people who have had literal visitations of demons in these forms. When I was a child, fear increased in my life by reading a certain fairy tale and viewing the pictures of a witch and her deeds. My fears also increased through another fairy tale and its accompanying music that was read on numerous occasions in my early school life. Small children are particularly vulnerable to fear through what they see and hear.

41

7. The Work of Demons

In John 10 Jesus describes Himself as the good shepherd — the one who cares for His sheep, who loves His sheep. In contrast, He spoke of the thief and the wolf, describing the work of Satan and his followers:

"I am the door; if anyone enters through Me, he shall be saved, and shall go in and out, and find pasture. The thief comes only to steal, and kill, and destroy; I came that they might have life, and might have it abundantly. I am the good shepherd; the good shepherd lays down His life for the sheep. He who is a hireling, and not a shepherd, who is not the owner of the sheep, beholds the wolf coming, and leaves the sheep, and flees, and the wolf snatches them, and scatters them."   *— Verses 9-12*

"The thief comes only to *steal*, and *kill*, and *destroy*." This summarizes the work of demons. What could be clearer? Demons will steal your health, your peace, your sanity, your patience. They are robbers! If you let them, they will literally take your physical life. Multitudes of Christians die before their allotted time. It is not God's will for a mother, for instance, to be robbed of her health and ultimately her life by some cancer, and leave her husband and sorrowing little children. Satan is a robber! A destroyer! A murderer! We must not let him continue to have his way so easily in our families.

During a school vacation, we conducted a series of meetings for children, instructing them on the Bible principles of deliverance. The boys and girls came with their parents and I endeavored to impart truth in a way they could understand. (Children have little difficulty with this realm. It is the older people, who have lost their childlikeness, that struggle over spiritual realities.) Speaking to the children, I said:

"When sickness comes to your home and someone in your family is suffering — is in great pain — Satan is happy, so happy. He loves to see people sick. He loves to see people miserable. He is excited when people are crying out in pain; when people are struggling for breath in an asthma attack. That's the kind of person he is. He is a horrible, horrible person!

"But Jesus is just the opposite. Jesus is sad if these things happen. He is full of love towards us. He wants us to be free from pain, free from sickness, free from sorrow. His heart is very, very sad. He wants to heal us, to make us well."

Let us be aware of the type of enemy we are dealing with.

42

Christians, we are at war! Not playing church! Not playing games! We are soldiers fighting an enemy who rests not day or night. The time for half-hearted Christianity is in the past. We are to rise in the power of God's Spirit, and successfully overcome the works of darkness.

8. The Names of Demons

A fine young woman came to me and asked if she should confess to the church that she had lied to various members and ask their forgiveness. For years she had lied to people unable to stop the habit. Even though she now had been a Christian for two years, she still had not been able to control the impulse to lie. But during the service the previous Sunday, she had been released from a lying spirit and now she was free to speak the truth.

This evil spirit had a name and a particular function to fulfill. It was a lying spirit whose function was to compel the young woman to lie. All evil spirits that come into our lives are like this. They have a name and a function.

One day someone came wanting to be delivered from spirits of pride — a rare thing because spirits of pride usually hinder the person from admitting his need. As we prayed naming the area, the spirits began to manifest. Use your imagination and think for a moment of someone that is proud and arrogant. Well, this is just how the spirits manifested. The person sat upright in the seat, puffed out her chest, lifted her head proudly, and began to sniff, sniff, sniff. It was so humorous that for a moment those of us counseling could not control our laughter.

The name of this spirit was pride, and its function was to make the person arrogant and aloof.

There are various names of spirits mentioned in the Bible. For example:

Unclean spirit	(Mark 1:23)
Deaf and dumb spirit	(Mark 9:25)
Blind and dumb spirit	(Matthew 12:22)
Spirit of sickness	(Luke 13:11)
Deceitful spirits	(1 Timothy 4:1)
Spirit of distortion	(Isaiah 19:14)
Spirit of harlotry	(Hosea 4:12)
Spirit of divination	(Acts 16:16)
Familiar spirits	(Leviticus 19:31 AV)

43

Through personal experience, through counseling and praying with many others, and through the operation of discernings of spirits, I have come to the conclusion that the list could go on indefinitely. **To list every type of demon, you would have to list every type of sin. Also there are spirits behind every negative emotion — fear, sorrow, loneliness, rejection, etc., etc.**

This does not mean that every negative emotional response stems from an evil spirit. Being sorrowful does not necessarily mean that you are bound by a spirit of sorrow. We all experience both positive and negative emotions. However, many people, through not knowing how to handle negative pressures, open themselves to spiritual bondage.

9. Families of Demons

Evil spirits do not as a rule work as individuals in a person's life. Rather they work together in families or groups.

If a person has a fear problem, the greater the fear, the stronger the hold and the more spirits involved in the bondage area. **Evil spirits gain their strength through their numbers**.

Under the general heading of fear there are many different kinds of fear. For instance, insecurity is a type of fear, as is inferiority, embarrassment, shyness, worry, anxiety, etc. Also there are multitudes of fears such as the fear of man, fear of failure, fear of disappointment, fear of loneliness, fear of death, fear of water, fear of animals, fear of authority, fear of the supernatural, fear of heights, etc., etc.

If a person has a stronghold of sorrow, working together in the sorrow family may be names such as regret, self-pity, anguish, and mourning.

If a person has a spirit of rejection, usually he has the fear of rejection as well. Loneliness may also be involved.

A person who has spirits of anger often needs release from frustration as well. Spirits works together. One opens the door to the other.

It is also important to realize that a person may have a number of exactly the same kind of spirit. For example, a person may have several spirits of acrophobia (fear of heights). The person comes for deliverance, receives prayer, spirits leave, and he goes away rejoicing, praising God for the victory, and continuing to walk in the ways of the Lord. Next week he goes mountain climbing and find that (to the same or to a lesser degree) he still has the problem. What does he do now? He may become discouraged, either concluding that deliverance doesn't work or that the spirits have returned. But if he knows that there can still be others of the same spirit remaining, then instead of being disheartened, he can rise up and come against them and press on to receive complete deliverance.

In Chapter 13 we will see that deliverance is a process and it may take much time to break down a whole family of spirits. In my own experience I had many deep deliverances in the same areas over extended periods. On some occasions I literally vomited so deeply while being released, that I thought there could not possibly be any more spirits left in that stronghold. And yet I had to continue pressing in to total freedom month after month. It was these experiences that taught me the strength and depth of some demonized areas. The stronger an area of bondage, the more spirits there are involved, and usually the longer the deliverance takes to complete.

Because demons work in families, I have found it best when dealing with them, to **speak in the singular**, but **think in the plural**.

In the Gospels a group of spirits can be referred to interchangeably as "spirit" (singular) or "spirits" (plural).

In Mark 5 we read the story of the Gerasene demoniac. Verse 2 says that a man . . . *with an unclean spirit [singular]* . . . met Jesus. In verse 7 again it is referred to in the singular: . . . *"What do I [singular] have to do with You, Jesus, Son of the Most High God? I [singular] implore You by God, do not torment me [singular]!"* But when the demon was asked its name, notice the switch from singular to plural: . . . *"My [singular] name is Legion; for we [plural] are many."* Verse 12: . . . *"Send us [plural] into the swine so that we [plural] may enter them."* Verse 13: *And He gave them [plural] permission. . . .*

In Mark 1:23-24 the Bible says the man had *an unclean spirit*, as if in the singular. But when the spirit spoke, it was speaking on behalf of many spirits, for it said, *"What do we [plural] have to do with You, Jesus of Nazareth? Have You come to destroy us [plural]? I [singular] know who You are — the Holy One of God!"*

In both these incidents there was a spokesman. Some spirits exercise more power and authority than others. Often I speak directly to the head of a family, to the key spirit, to the leader of the group, and thus get right to the core of the stronghold.

10. The Defeat and Destiny of Demons

In Chapter 4 we looked at the defeat and destiny of Satan and saw that Satan and his angels and all of humanity that do not turn to Christ are destined to eternal punishment in the lake of fire. Demons share this same destiny.

In Matthew's account of the Gerasene demoniac, the demons in the man cried out, . . . *"What do we have to do with You, Son of God? Have You come here to torment us before the time?"* *(8:29).* The demons knew the authority of Jesus Christ and that at the appointed time He would assign them to their eternal abode of judgment.

From time to time when spirits are very stubborn and resisting the commands to go, I remind them they have been eternally defeated by Jesus Christ, and the more they torment a child of God, the more will be their torment in the lake of fire.

Where, you may ask, do demons go when they are cast out? Can we assign them to hell? Sometimes people command spirits to go to the pit or to some other place. From the Word of God we have no direction to give such commands. Jesus Himself never gave them. He simply cast them out. On one occasion He told them never to return (Mark 9:25).

Matthew 12:43-45 tells us that when spirits are cast out they pass through waterless or dry places seeking rest. They either look for a new home or seek to return to the one they came from. This does not mean we need fear that evil spirits will return. [See Chapter 17.]

11. Casting Out Demons

Once we know about demons, what are we to do about them? The answer is simple: If they have already found a place in our life, we are to *cast them out.* If they are seeking a place in our life, we are to *keep them out.*

Who is to cast our demons? Jesus cast out demons (Mark 1:39); the twelve disciples cast out demons (Matthew 10:1); the seventy cast out demons (Luke 10:17); and all believers are to cast out demons (Mark 16:17).

How are we to cast them out? Casting out demons is not a meek and mild kind of thing. We do not cast them out by saying politely, "Demon, will you please leave." We are dealing with rebellious, vile, stubborn, wicked creatures. They are to be violently expelled.

The Greek word *ekballo*, translated "cast out," is very expressive. Its root *ballo* means "to throw or hurl." *Ekballo* means "eject, cast forth, cast out, drive out, expel, pluck out, pull out, take out, thrust out, put out, send away, send out."

In everyday usage *cast* means "to throw or expel with violence or force," and *out* means "at or to a point beyond the limits of some location." In Jesus' name, therefore, we are to violently expel evil spirits out of their place or location. As we do this, a righteous indignation is to fill our hearts. It is warfare! It is not sitting back passively, but rising up aggressively in the power of the Holy Spirit.

Let us see how the word *ekballo* is used in other contexts in the Bible:

In the Nazareth synagogue, after Jesus had read and explained Isaiah's prophecy, the people . . . *were filled with rage . . . and they rose up and cast Him out of the city, and led Him to the brow of the hill . . . in order to throw Him down the cliff (Luke 4:28-29).*

When Stephen gave his defense before the council, his words so angered the people that *they cried out with a loud voice, and covered their ears, and they rushed upon him with one impulse. And when they had driven him out of the city, they began stoning him . . . (Acts 7:57-58).*

When Jesus entered the temple in Jerusalem, He was filled with righteous indignation that His Father's house had become a house of merchandise: *And He made a scourge of cords, and drove them all out of the temple . . . (John 2:15).*

Can we see Jesus, gripped by the zeal of God, a scourge of cords in His hand, driving out (ekballo-ing) the merchandisers? Can we see Stephen driven out (ekballo-ed) of the city by violent men to be murdered? Can we see the Jews rising with rage and casting (ekballo-ing) Jesus out of Nazareth to throw Him down a cliff to His death?

In this same manner, we are told to cast out (ekballo) demons. We are to be violently aggressive, in the zeal and anointing of God, against the works of darkness.

12. The Price of Casting Out Demons

A definition of price is: the cost at which anything is obtained. To be involved in a regular way in casting out demons brings an expenditure of time and strength. To meet the demands of spiritual warfare, one has to be renewed constantly through fellowship with God and reading His Word.

But this is only part of the cost. There is another price which has to be paid by many who set others free. It is the cost of being faced with discredit and all sorts of accusations. Attacks often come through fellow believers who are blinded to the subtle workings of the enemy and feel they are doing God a service by speaking against such things. In dealing with demons, we are exposing and tearing down Satan's inroads in lives. This is the last thing Satan wants. No wonder he gets upset. Casting out demons is sure to be a controversial issue. Satan will see to that.

Jesus Himself came under attack for casting out demons. In Mark 3:10-11 we read that when Jesus was healing and delivering, spirits were falling down (through human bodies) before Him, and acknowledging He was the Son of God. Then we read of His appointing the twelve disciples and giving them authority to cast out demons (verses 14-19). The next thing we read is what happened when He returned home to His own kinsmen: When they heard of His coming, . . . *they went out to take custody of Him; for they were saying, "He has lost His senses" (verse 21).* Imagine going home to your family and friends and being told you were deranged! Out of your mind! Lost your senses! This is what Jesus faced, but what could have been further from the truth!

The next verse tells us what the scribes were saying about Him. Verse 22: *And the scribes who came down from Jerusalem were saying, "He is possessed by Beelzebul," and "He casts out the demons by the ruler of the demons."* Jesus was accused of being in league with Satan, the very one to whom He was totally opposed. He was accused of using Satan's power — not the power of the Holy Spirit — to cast out spirits.

This was a serious accusation, and a very serious thing for those who were making it. It is in this context that we read of the blasphemy of the Holy Spirit, a sin which the Bible calls an eternal sin and a sin from which there is no forgiveness (verses 28-30).

Let me say again: Satan will do all he can to hinder believers from casting out his "fifth column." He will send spirits of unbelief, intellectualism, prejudice, fear of man, violence, hatred, and so on, to distract the soldier of God from enforcing Calvary's victory. Don't look for opposition, but when it comes, don't be surprised. It may come openly or it may come in a quiet, subtle way. But in whatever way it comes, don't forget to rejoice.

Blessed are you when men cast insults at you, and persecute you, and say all kinds of evil against you falsely, on account of Me.

48

Rejoice, and be glad, for your reward in heaven is great, for so they persecuted the prophets who were before you. — *Matthew 5:11-12*

Paul and Silas were thrown into prison for casting a spirit of divination out of a slave-girl, but in prison they sang hymns of praise to God (Acts 16:16-25).

Be careful, however, that the opposition is not because you are acting in the flesh and lacking in wisdom and tact. To act foolishly is to deserve opposition. But if the opposition comes because you are moving in the Holy Spirit, REJOICE!

Chapter 6

The Entrance of Demons

There are different ways in which demons can enter our lives. By becoming familiar with these, we can be on our guard to prevent their entry.

1. During Pregnancy

Evil spirits are frequently transferred from parents to child even before the child is born.

While praying one day for a mother for deliverance, her three-month-old baby, who was with us in the room, began to cry increasingly. This often happens. The enemy tries to distract sessions of prayer by disturbing the children. Normally I try not to be distracted, but this time I felt led to pray for the child. I sensed spirits of rejection and began commanding them to leave. As they left, the baby yawned repeatedly very widely, much to the mother's surprise. She had never seen her baby yawn like this.

It may seem strange that a three-month-old baby would have spirits of rejection, especially a baby that had been born into a good home with parents who had welcomed the birth and dearly loved the child. In this case the mother herself had a stronghold of rejection and the spirits had been transferred to the child while it was forming in the womb.

I would say that today by far the majority of children are born into the world already demonized. Non-Christian parents can do little or nothing to hinder some transference taking place because their lives are under the dominion of the god of this world. In the case of Christian parents, if they themselves are completely free from all demonic bondage or if they know how to stand against the works of the enemy, transference can be avoided. However, to date, I see very few parents who are in this position.

I am not saying that every problem parents have will necessarily be transferred to their children, but I am saying that some spirits from problem areas certainly are.

Have you ever noticed how certain weaknesses, sins, and sicknesses are carried down through family lines? This is exactly what God said would happen when people turn from Him: . . . *I, the Lord your God, am a jealous God, visiting the iniquity of the fathers on the children, on the third and the fourth generations of those who hate Me (Exodus 20:5).*

Bondages are passed from generation to generation: lines of hatred, anger, physical or mental diseases, the inability to believe, and so on. If forebears have been involved in forms of witchcraft, there is most certainly some inherited bondage. We tend to accept family weaknesses as something we have to live with. Remarks of this kind are often made: "Oh, your father was like that and so was your grandfather." "She has her mother's temper." "Epilepsy has been in the family for generations." There are also bondages that exist at a national level — national traits that are carried down from generation to generation.

While worshipping the Lord one night in a gathering of Christian friends, the Holy Spirit spontaneously moved in a flow of deliverance. We encouraged those who were not experiencing deliverance to pray for those who were. In response a young university student prayed for the person alongside her. As she prayed, she herself suddenly began to have manifestations. Finding it difficult to breathe, she ran from the room, and collapsed unconscious outside. After trying without success to rouse her, we carried her back into the meeting and everyone gathered around praising God for His presence and power; but she did not regain consciousness. At the end of the meeting, Shirley continued to minister to her, and eventually she rallied. When she was free, she told us that a spirit had spoken within her saying that its name was deception and that it had come from her grandfather and was not going to leave.

This young woman had had a history of repeatedly going well in her faith, then wavering. At one stage, we thought she would lose her faith completely. Something within had often tried to deceive her and draw her aside. It was a spirit that had originated from her grandfather and been transferred down through the family line. Today she is strong and sure in her faith.

Spirits that are transferred do not necessarily begin their work immediately. They may lie dormant for many years before they rise to manifest. For example, a spirit of infidelity may be transferred to a child in the womb, but will not manifest until adult years when it then rises up to breach faithfulness within the marriage relationship.

A Christian with leadership responsibilities came to me seeking counsel. When we prayed I discerned spirits of insanity and together we began to name, bind, and break up what was a major stronghold. As we did so, the spirits manifested, twisting the man's face and body into some of the most grotesque expressions I have ever seen. His face looked like that of a completely insane person; he slobbered; his arms and hands were bent and shaking. Even when we had times of rest in the midst of the warfare, he could not make his face relax. Later he told me that on his mother's side of the family was a history of mental deficiency. He himself, although outwardly normal, had within him the potential for severe mental breakdown. The evil spirits had been lying dormant waiting an opportunity to seek to do their work.

When we are born of the Spirit of God, we are legally severed from evil things passed on to us from our ancestors. We become new creations in Christ. We are no longer of the inheritance of Adam, but of the inheritance of Christ. At times, when the Holy Spirit guides, I pray like this: "Lord, we break this bondage. We break every inherited factor to the third and fourth generation. This believer is no longer in Adam, but in Christ. The power of sin has been broken. We are new creations in Christ. Every evil spirit that has come through the family line, we break your power now."

During a deliverance meeting, I was led by the Spirit to break the inherited power of insanity to the third and fourth generations. Without warning, two people were thrown from their seats, one person almost into the row behind. Deep and hidden holds had been touched by the finger of God, the Holy Spirit; and the demons, startled and in fear, suddenly manifested.

We have said that demons frequently enter while a child is forming in the womb. Another time at which the door is often opened, is during the birth itself. For some babies, birth is traumatic, especially a difficult instrumental birth. It seems that from the earliest moment a son of Adam enters the world, demons are there seeking to rob, kill, and destroy. They take advantage of every situation they can to do their evil work.

As parents, we are not to be afraid or feel guilty because of what we may have transferred to our children. Don't allow the enemy a place for self-condemnation, but use truth to overcome him. Let us press through to freedom, praying both for ourselves and for our children. Let us enter into the blessings of Christ's inheritance gained at Calvary, when He legally broke Satan's power over the human race. Let's declare to bondages which go back in the family line that the price of the precious Blood has been paid for our freedom; that by faith we are now in Christ, in the kingdom of light; and that old things have passed away. 2 Corinthians 5:17.

2. Through Sin

If as believers, or as unbelievers, we give ourselves to any sin, we give legal ground for demons to gain a measure of control in our lives in the area or areas involved; whether that sin be resentment, anger, immorality, or whatever. There are serious consequences for continuing in sin.

When we obey God, a hedge of protection is around our lives, but when we disobey, a breach is made in the hedge.

Job, a righteous man who feared God and turned from evil (Job 1:8), had a hedge of protection around him that prevented Satan touching him. Satan said to God, *"Hast Thou not made a hedge about him and his house and all that he has, on every side? Thou hast blessed the work of his hands, and his possessions have increased in the land" (Job 1:10).*

Isaiah 5 likens the nation of Israel to a vineyard which God planted with good seed and around which He built a hedge and a wall. But Israel sinned and turned away from Jehovah and His statutes. As a result, God said: . . . *"I will remove its hedge and it will be consumed; I will break down its wall and it will become trampled ground. And I will lay it waste; It will not be pruned or hoed, But briars and thorns will come up. I will also charge the clouds to rain no rain on it" (verses 5-6).*

When the wall of protection is taken down, or when even one small opening is made in the wall, a place is given for evil spirits to enter and do their destroying work. The Christian life is not a game. We cannot play with sin or demons.

Romans 6 tells us that when we yield to sin, we become slaves to sin. A slave is powerless to break free; he has to obey his master. By giving ourselves to sin, we open the way for demon powers to come in and enslave us to the sin we gave ourselves to. In contrast, we can

54

yield ourselves to righteousness and become slaves to God. Slavery to sin or slavery to God. We choose.

Deuteronomy 28 speaks of numerous blessings and cursings. Of the sixty-eight verses in the chapter, only fourteen speak of the blessings that overtake God's people through their obedience to the commandments of the Lord. Walking in God's ways opens the door to positive provisions. These embrace honor, increase, fruitfulness, victory, holiness, health, etc.

But then there are fifty-four verses that declare the cursings that overtake God's people through disobedience. These cursings are numerous. They include defeat by our enemies, every kind of sickness and disease, mental breakdowns, breaking up of families, hunger, fear, despair, and so on. When we fool with sin, we come under the influence of the curse. Take time to read this chapter.

A group of Christian teenage girls were being tempted to do something they knew was wrong. One lass said, "Come on, let's do it. God is a God of forgiveness and after we've committed the sin, we can ask Him to forgive us." What a foolish and careless attitude! What lack of repentance! Fortunately the girls did not pursue their course of action. One of them later related the incident to us.

There are three reasons why I choose not to sin: (a) the fear of the Lord, (b) the principle of sowing and reaping, and (c) the fact that sin gives legal ground for demons to enter.

(a) The Fear of the Lord

I trust this is my purest motive. I love the Lord and honor Him and desire to please Him, having a holy sense of awe at His greatness and might.

The fear of the Lord is to hate evil; Pride and arrogance and the evil way, And the perverted mouth, I hate. — Proverbs 8:13

(b) Sowing and Reaping

There is a divine principle of sowing and reaping. It is a natural as well as a spiritual principle. When living in a wheat-belt area of Australia, several times I deliberately counted the number of grains of wheat in the heads of stools. From a single grain planted, I have counted as many as eight hundred grains produced.

When we sow, we reap. We reap what we sow, and we reap more than we sow. In the natural realm there may be crop failures, but never in the spiritual realm. There may be times when we appear not to reap, yet we can be sure that a harvest will eventually follow. In the natural realm some seeds, for example, radish, produce a harvest in a very short time; whereas other seeds take months or even years before there is a harvest. The same is true in the spiritual realm: our reaping may be soon, later, or continuous.

Sowing and reaping is not just a negative principle. As we sow good seeds in daily actions of love and righteousness, we will reap a good harvest; for we reap what we sow, and we reap more than we sow.

Do not be deceived, God is not mocked; for whatever a man sows, this he will also reap. For the one who sows to his own flesh shall from the flesh reap corruption, but the one who sows to the Spirit shall from the Spirit reap eternal life. — *Galatians 6:7-8*

2 Samuel 24 relates the story of David sinning against the Lord in numbering Israel. When Joab, who had tried to dissuade the king, returned with the tally, David's heart troubled him, and he . . . *said to the Lord, "I have sinned greatly in what I have done. But now, O Lord, please take away the iniquity of Thy servant, for I have acted very foolishly" (verse 10).* Although God forgave David, this sin brought a great reaping to Israel: seventy thousand men died (verse 15).

It does not matter how spiritual we are, the principle of sowing and reaping still applies. In fact, the greater the light we turn from, the greater the judgment can be.

Speaking of David, we know well of his reaping in relation to his adultery with Bathsheba (2 Samuel 11). One act of adultery led him into deceit and murder, and a great and continuing harvest of judgments. Nathan the prophet was the instrument through whom the Lord exposed David's sin; but only after David had condemned himself through judging the rich man's action on the poor man who had only one ewe lamb. David said, . . . *"As the Lord lives, surely the man who has done this deserves to die. And he must make restitution for the lamb fourfold, because he did this thing and had no compassion" (2 Samuel 12:5-6).*

David certainly reaped fourfold:

1. *The sword shall never depart from your house (verse 10).*
2. *I will raise up evil against you from your own household (verse 11).*
3. *I will even take your wives before your eyes, and give them to your companion, and he shall lie with your wives in broad daylight (verse 11).*

4. *The child also that is born to you [by Bathsheba] shall surely die (verse 14).*

The following chapters unfold the awful consequences of David's sin as these words come to pass. Because David repented, the Lord took away his sin (verse 13) promising him he would not die; yet although forgiven, he still had to reap sin's consequences.

(c) Legal Ground for Demons

You may go through all the religious motions of righteousness; you may fool your pastor and friends; but if you are deliberately continuing in sin, you have a sign on the door of your house inviting new tenants. It reads: "ROOMS VACANT." The Bible warns us not to give place to the devil (Ephesians 4:27).

John 5 tells of Jesus healing a man who had been sick for thirty-eight years. After raising him, Jesus slipped away in the crowd; but later He found him in the temple and said, . . . *"Behold, you have become well; do not sin anymore, so that nothing worse may befall you" (verse 14).* The Amplified New Testament says plainly, . . . *"Stop sinning, or something worse may happen to you."*

Sin not only has consequences physically, as in this case, but also mentally, emotionally, and spiritually.

Before turning wholeheartedly to Christ, I had given myself to unclean speech. Through my high school years I had the reputation of being clean, and one who did not appreciate the unclean stories and remarks of my school mates. I was respected for my stand. But after six months in the merchant navy, I had developed a very foul tongue which often embarrassed even my fellow seamen when I was ashore in the company of others. I had come to a place where at times I was unaware of what I was saying. Unclean expressions would pour from me. When I came to Christ, although my speech was changed, the problem continued in my thoughts. For years I battled against curse and swear words in my mind that made me feel terribly condemned. These thoughts particularly arose at times when I was being exercised in spiritual responses such as worship. When I finally recognized the source as demonic, I was able to begin to cleanse my mind. One day during spiritual warfare, the Lord quickened my memory and showed me when the first of these spirits found a place.

When I was a small boy playing with other children in a neighbor's yard, I was dared to swear at the top of my voice. The pressure was great and I finally succumbed, thus violating the teachings of my parents, but even worse, violating my own conscience. I became extremely guilty, and returned home sure that my parents had heard. But they hadn't. Although I never swore again until my days as a seaman, this act of sin opened the door to spirits of unclean speech. They then waited patiently till they could freely manifest themselves. Other spirits joined them, and this area became a stronghold. How foolish to think that we can sin and not suffer!

A friend sought prayer because of a weight problem. She was a farmer's wife and spent much time in the kitchen preparing meals for her husband and the workers, and could not stop constantly picking at food. She was putting on so much weight that her clothes were not fitting. As we talked, we discovered her problem began through the sin of pride and criticism.

Her pastor's wife was a large woman with an uncontrolled appetite. While she greedily ate at a church function, our friend had mocked her in her heart and prided herself at her own control. She then began to criticize. From that moment a desire for food overcame her, and she found herself eating excessively. As we spoke on repentance and confession, she willingly confessed her sin and received forgiveness by faith. Then she renounced the spirit of gluttony and was set free. Soon she returned to her normal weight.

We also discovered that she had not been baptized in water even though the Lord had been speaking to her about it for three years. She confessed this disobedience as sin, and within a week was baptized. As she came out of the water, she experienced a further inward releasing. Obedience brings blessings.

One of the most common ways in which legal ground is given to the enemy is by harboring unforgiveness and resentment. Whatever the sin, repent! For your own sake, repent! Choose to walk in the light. We must will daily to walk close to Jesus whatever the cost. Not to, is even more costly.

3. Through Emotional Crises

Demons take advantage of any crisis time. Without sinning, a person can be overwhelmed and come into bondage, all because he did not know how to keep himself in a time of distress.

A person who nearly drowns may come into bondage to a fear of water; a person attacked by a dog may open to a fear of dogs; a person in a car accident may open to a fear of driving; a person bereaved of a loved one may open to spirits of grief; a child left alone in a house may open to spirits of loneliness; a person with a serious illness may open to a spirit of death. Life is fraught with crises, great and small. How we go through them determines liberty or bondage.

In a deliverance meeting, while I was praying over the congregation breaking bondages as the Lord guided me, a pastor's wife sitting in the front row was receiving much deliverance. I discerned that it was in the area of fear. A little later, I moved towards her and was led in the Spirit to break the fear of thunderstorms. After the meeting she told me that her earliest recollections of life were of being held in her mother's arms, hiding under the bed during thunderstorms. Her mother was petrified of thunder and lightning. This little child had not sinned, but was unprotected at times of crisis and demons took advantage of it.

Already I have shared of a major crisis in my own life at the age of six which greatly fashioned my personality negatively. I had to receive much deliverance from spirits which entered my life at that time. There were also many other incidents that the Lord quickened to me as He taught me to set myself free.

Comedy always tickles a sensitive spot in me. As a child I loved characters such as Laurel and Hardy and attended every one of their movies that I possibly could. Roaring with laughter, I would intensely enjoy their antics. In one film, however, I recall my heroes being trapped in a cave with crocodiles after them. I was too young to handle the emotional trauma. Hurriedly I left the theatre and stood shaking on the pavement outside. I can see now that this caused a further foothold of fear to be gained in my life.

Parents, I urge you, without being over-protective, to be on guard for your children, especially the younger ones. Millions of youngsters give place to demons while they sit watching TV programs. As they view violence and disrespect for authority, if they consent to what they watch, they can open themselves to spirits in those areas. Others receive frights and become bound by fear as I did. Let us not be afraid of the enemy, but aware of his tactics. Life is not a game, an endless amusement park. We are at war!

Another cause of emotional trauma to children (and adults) is being called names. The old saying, "Sticks and stones may break my bones, but names will never hurt me," is not true. When a child or adult is called names or teased, unless he knows the protection that Jesus affords, he becomes hurt and can open himself to spirits of rejection, disappointment, failure, etc. Continually being called names or being left out of activities can cause hurts that give the enemy ground for entry. Constant criticism can also have the same effect.

If we find ourselves in a crisis, we should keep our eyes on the Lord Jesus, be aware of what demons will try to do, and hold fast a confession of victory in the midst of the pressures. Should the enemy gain a hold, we should smartly rebuke him and set ourselves free.

4. Through Ignorance

All too often demons gain entrance through ignorance. Not knowing the tactics of these opposing spiritual powers, and not seeing them with the natural eye, we can easily live as if they were not there.

A young minister sought counsel from us. While looking to the Lord for direction, we felt led to break bondages of depression and self-pity. We then discovered that before he was converted, he used to pull the drapes to darken his room, select morbid music, and lie on the floor feeling sorry for himself. In ignorance he had opened himself to evil spirits.

While ministering to a sick woman in a meeting, I discerned a spirit of death. Upon rebuking it, she collapsed to the floor and was set free. Later she asked me when it had entered. Not knowing, I told her to have her heart open, and perhaps the Lord would show her. A few days later, she informed me she had her answer. Five years previously her father had died, and in her sorrow some days after his death, she had cried out that she wished she were dead. In her ignorance she had given ground to the enemy by a negative confession.

Whenever spirits of death are discerned, I ask the person if he has ever pondered or desired death. If he has (which is often the case), I lead him in a renunciation of his former speech or attitudes; ask him to confess Jesus to be his life, and to choose to live and follow Jesus as the resurrection and the life; and then ask him to renounce the spirit of death.

Having a spirit of death, does not mean a person is dead. Rather, he has a spirit which will attempt to cut short his life span. It will often work in association with spirits such as infirmity or suicide.

It is imperative that we keep ourselves protected in times of bereavement. Although it is natural to be sorrowful when a loved one dies (and there is nothing wrong with this), it is important that we have on the armor of God. Any demons that were in the deceased person will be seeking a new home. The closest place for them to look is in the family members, and because of excessive grief, they often have an open door. During times of stress we must be aware of the enemy's tactics and lean on God's keeping power.

While teaching at a church school, I witnessed the funeral of a student's grandmother. The student's mother, overwhelmed with grief, cried out so loudly and uncontrollably that the family members had to physically restrain her. I felt sorry for her because I knew what was happening in the unseen realm.

The enemy takes advantage of our ignorance. Let's be informed so he cannot sneak up on us.

5. Through Parental Default

Within a Christian family protection is afforded the children as the husband and wife live in harmony with one another before the Lord, and exercise a loving influence. Parents are to set an atmosphere in the home where peace and love abound and children feel secure. Children are to be taught and trained in the ways of God.

Ephesians 6:4 says that fathers are to . . . *bring them up [that is, "to rear up to maturity"] in the discipline and instruction of the Lord*. The Greek words translated *discipline* and *instruction* speak of "training by word" and "training by act."

Parents have a responsibility to fulfill the commandments of God in respect to their children. Through their diligence, they can spare their children many problems and keep them from demonic infiltration.

I recall helping a young person troubled by a fear of being attacked. He had developed this fear through seeing his father constantly strike his mother. Whenever anyone near him raised a hand or arm, he immediately drew back fearfully taking a defensive posture even though nothing negative was intended. This was bondage caused through a parent defaulting.

Recently I witnessed a child throwing an extreme tantrum because he could not get his own way with the other children. The Christian father intervened, but allowed the child to continue in a state of rage, taking no corrective action even though the child was causing a disturbance to other people nearby. The father seemed helpless. The child was in control, not the father. I believe this father was defaulting. Firm control should have been taken to stop the tantrum, and instruction given on not doing such a thing and having right responses. Spirits of anger, jealousy, etc., can enter at times like this. When

61

praying for older people to be delivered from these kinds of spirits, I have witnessed the spirits manifest with fits of temper and throwing tantrums.

Tension between parents, critical and destructive words, lack of attention and care, and numerous other negative situations place a child in danger of demonic attack and infiltration. There is much helpful literature available today on the Christian family, which parents would be wise to read.

6. Through Occult Involvement

When a person identifies with any form of the occult, whether deliberately or in curiosity, he is endangering himself. The Scriptures clearly tell us not to be involved and warns us of the consequences:

When you enter the land which the Lord your God gives you, you shall not learn to imitate the detestable things of those nations. There shall not be found among you anyone who makes his son or his daughter pass through the fire, one who uses divination, one who practices witchcraft, or one who interprets omens, or a sorcerer, or one who casts a spell, or a medium, or a spiritist, or one who calls up the dead. For whoever does these things is detestable to the Lord; and because of these detestable things the Lord your God will drive them out before you. You shall be blameless before the Lord your God. For those nations, which you shall dispossess, listen to those who practice witchcraft and to diviners, but as for you, the Lord your God has not allowed you to do so. — *Deuteronomy 18:9-14.*

Divination is seeking revelation by supernatural means other than by the Holy Spirit. Witchcraft or sorcery is affecting people or bringing them under control through the use of spells, curses, hypnoses, charms, music, drugs, etc.

If you have been in any form of occult involvement, you must confess it to the Lord and renounce every evil spirit that has found access into your life because of it. To step into this realm is to step into collaboration with Satan and his purposes. Those who have been deeply involved often have major battles to become completely free.

The book of Leviticus also gives firm warnings against occult involvement:

Do not turn to mediums or spiritists; do not seek them out to be defiled by them. I am the Lord your God. — *Leviticus 19:31*

As for the person who turns to mediums and to spiritists, to play the harlot after them, I will also set My face against that person and will cut him off from among his people.   *— Leviticus 20:6*

Today things of the occult have become "popular." Practices once frowned upon and done in secret are now openly exposed to invite and trap the unwary. Books and occult objects can be bought in stores, and people of all ages are being deceived and distracted further away from the truth and life that can only be found in Christ. We need to turn from and break association with all companions and objects that are of this realm.

In Acts 19 we read of those who turned to Christ from the ways of the occult: *Many also of those who had believed kept coming, confessing and disclosing their practices. And many of those who practiced magic brought their books together and began burning them in the sight of all; and they counted up the price of them and found it fifty thousand pieces of silver (verses 18-19).*

Even if we have not been willfully involved in occult practices, occult books or objects in our homes can bring us under a measure of satanic influence. One evening while visiting Christian friends, I sensed a demonic presence in their home. Then I noticed that in the corner of the lounge room were numerous Papua New Guinean souvenirs and artifacts that had been associated with demonic rituals; and I became aware that the evil presence went back to these objects. A few days later I shared with the couple how I had felt, and encouraged them to destroy the artifacts. Together they decided this was a right course of action, and removed the objects from the house. Immediately a heaviness lifted that had hovered over the home for twenty years, and the family members came into new liberty within themselves.

Many Christians bring home souvenirs from holiday resorts or mission stations not realizing that things like fetishes, and carvings of gods or animals that are worshipped, have evil spirits associated with them. We must destroy and break all association with such things.

The realm of witchcraft extends further than many people realize. It involves anything that is an attempt to control people and have them do what you want by spiritual powers other than the Holy Spirit. It is possible for a parent to dominate a child, a husband a wife, or a pastor a congregation, without their being aware that in their effort to control situations, they are releasing spiritual powers other than the Holy Spirit. There is a God-appointed leadership and strength that must be exercised, but we must not step beyond our God-ordained responsibilities into cooperation with demonic activity. If we do, we move into the area of withcraft.

I know a middle-aged Christian woman who lives at home with her Christian parents. As a child her mother dominated her and now still dominates her life to such a degree that she is incapable of living without "mother" and could never be married and live a normal life. She is under heavy domination and has never been allowed to grow up. Her mother is a witch although she would no doubt be horrified if confronted with such a charge.

There was a period in our lives when we attended a church that was dominated by a well-meaning pastor. Void of the Holy Spirit's anointing, he did all in his "soul" power to enforce his legalistic standards of holiness. Consequently there was a heaviness over the church, and many members lived in fear because of his heavy handedness in the name of God. We always left Sunday services under a cloud of discouragement, and I don't remember ever being edified by his ministry. Unconsciously, this dear pastor was releasing a ministry of demonic activity among the people, resulting in spiritual death rather than spiritual life.

It is also possible to be under the domination of a person or persons with whom one has had past illicit sexual relationships. We have released many people from this kind of domination. The bondages were either hindering the developing of a normal healthy sexual relationship within marriage, or hindering the person from being able to commence a friendship that would lead to marriage.

If we are guilty of dominating, we need to repent and claim release from all demonic powers that have operated through us. If we have been dominated, we need to rise up in faith and declare our release. Often this will involve decisive steps of breaking from under those by whom we have been controlled. We need God-given wisdom to know how best to do this, especially when it involves family members.

Let us break from every association with the occult realm so as to give no ground for evil spirits to bind. We belong to the kingdom of light, and are called to walk in the light.

Chapter 7

Spiritual Equipment for Spiritual Warfare

While in this world, we live in the midst of the conflict between the kingdom of God and the kingdom of darkness. We can praise God that as Christians we are on the winning side. Jesus Christ has already declared victory on our behalf. Satan and his hosts are already defeated. Our fighting is not to win the battle, but to enforce the already-won victory. Jesus has done His part; now He is looking to us to do our part. We are to be His soldiers.

Soldiers need both armor and weapons. In our spiritual war, we need spiritual armor and spiritual weapons — not natural ones. We cannot fight a spiritual war with natural weapons. The Bible says: *For though we walk in the flesh, we do not war according to the flesh, for the weapons of our warfare are not of the flesh, but divinely powerful for the destruction of fortresses (2 Corinthians 10:3-4).*

Jesus Christ has given to His church armor for protection and weapons for defense and offense. This equipment is "divinely powerful." It is the best that we could have, and absolutely adequate to meet every onslaught of the enemy. It never needs updating as does equipment for natural warfare. The church today has available to it the same equipment as the early church had.

Let us first consider our spiritual armor and then our spiritual weapons:

The Armor of God

Finally, be strong in the Lord, and in the strength of His might. Put on the full armor of God, that you may be able to stand firm against the schemes of the devil. For our struggle is not against flesh and blood, but against the rulers, against the powers, against the world forces of this darkness, against the spiritual forces of wickedness in the heavenly places.

Therefore, take up the full armor of God, that you may be able to resist in the evil day, and having done everything, to stand firm.

Stand firm therefore, having girded your loins with truth, and having put on the breastplate of righteousness, and having shod your feet with the preparation of the gospel of peace; in addition to all, taking up the shield of faith with which you will be able to extinguish all the flaming missiles of the evil one. And take the helmet of salvation, and the sword of the Spirit, which is the word of God. With all prayer and petition pray at all times in the Spirit, and with this in view, be on the alert with all perseverance and petition for all the saints. — Ephesians 6:10-18

God's Word exhorts us to "put on the full armor of God" — not just some pieces, but all of it.

There was a time when religiously every morning I put on the armor of God. But then one day I realized that if I were having to put it on in the morning, I must be taking it off at night. Now, constantly I simply thank the Lord that it is on. I keep it on all the time. I need it day and night.

In learning how to put it on, it helped me to realize that Jesus Himself is my armor:

The night is almost gone, and the day is at hand. Let us therefore lay aside the deeds of darkness and put on the armor of light. Let us behave properly as in the day, not in carousing and drunkenness, not in sexual promiscuity and sensuality, not in strife and jealousy. But put on the Lord Jesus Christ, and make no provision for the flesh in regard to its lusts. — Romans 13:12-14.

In these verses "putting on the armor of light" is equated with "putting on the Lord Jesus Christ." Other verses bring out this same idea: Galatians 3:27; Colossians 3:10.

By "putting on Jesus," "clothing myself with Christ," I am putting on the armor. Jesus is to me every part of the armor:

Truth (girdle): *Jesus said to him, "I am the way, and the truth, and the life; no one comes to the Father, but through Me" (John 14:6).*
Righteousness (breastplate): *But by His doing you are in Christ Jesus, who became to us wisdom from God, and righteousness and sanctification, and redemption (1 Corinthians 1:30).*
Peace (shoes): *Peace I leave with you; My peace I give to you; not as the world gives, do I give to you. Let not your heart be troubled, nor let it be fearful (John 14:27).*

Faith (shield): *Fixing our eyes on Jesus, the author and perfecter of faith, who for the joy set before Him endured the cross, despising the shame, and has sat down at the right hand of the throne of God (Hebrews 12:2).*

Salvation (helmet): *For it was fitting for Him, for whom are all things, and through whom are all things, in bringing many sons to glory, to perfect the author of their salvation through sufferings (Hebrews 2:10).*

Word of God (sword): *In the beginning was the Word, and the Word was with God, and the Word was God . . . And the Word became flesh, and dwelt among us, and we beheld His glory, glory as of the only begotten from the Father, full of grace and truth (John 1:1, 14).*

We put on our armor by a simple confession of faith: "Lord Jesus, You are my armor. You are my salvation. You are my hope (1 Thessalonians 5:8). You are my righteousness. You are my peace. You are my truth. You are the source of my faith. I am kept by Your Word. You are my very life. I stand this day in total protection from every attack of the enemy. In You I am strong. In You I am more than a conqueror."

Having put on our armor, we need to keep it on by a daily confession of faith, acknowledging Christ to be what each piece of armor represents. Then, with all our armor on, we are to resist our enemy and stand firm against him. Whether we are the weakest or the strongest believer, we are kept because of the armor of God — not because of human ability. It's the armor!

The Weapons of Warfare

God has equipped us with "divinely powerful" weapons to wield against the enemy. They are keys that unlock prison doors and set us free from enemy holds.

To be effective, each weapon must be used with faith. Faith releases them. In our Christian life *we walk by faith, not by sight (2 Corinthians 5:7).* We can go through the motions of using weapons, but if we lack faith, we will be ineffective.

Acts 19:13-16 tells of some Jewish exorcists who were attempting to cast out evil spirits in the name of the Lord Jesus whom Paul was preaching. They had the right formula, but no personal knowledge of salvation and no faith. Their efforts ended in disaster. The man with the evil spirits attacked them and overpowered them, and they fled stripped naked and wounded.

Because faith is so important, we shall consider it in detail in the next chapter. At this point, however, do not fear that you will not have sufficient faith to operate the weapons. Faith is not something for a select few. Every Christian has a measure of faith, and can learn how to release that measure and how to increase it. Romans 10:17 tells us that we receive faith through hearing. Even now as you hear of the weapons God has given you, faith can be coming to your heart.

1. The Name of the Lord Jesus Christ

I learned the power of the name of Jesus at the first encounter I ever had with demons. When I was a very young Christian, a young man who was having demonic manifestations approached a friend and me and asked us to pray for him. In our youthful zeal, we commanded the spirits to leave, declaring to them that they had no right to be there. The spirits manifested and called out, "You have no power over us! You have no power over us!"

We stopped and thought for a moment. "That's right," we said. "We don't have any power over them. It's Jesus who has the power." Then we changed our command and said, "In the name of Jesus, come out!" With this there was a turning of the tide.

When Peter and John healed the lame man at the Beautiful Gate of the temple, the people came to them amazed, thinking that Peter and John themselves had healed the man. But Peter said, ... *"Men of Israel, why do you marvel at this, or why do you gaze at us, as if by our own power or piety we had made him walk? . . . It is the name of Jesus which has strengthened this man whom you see and know"* . . . *(Acts 3:12, 16).*

In Philippians 2:8-11 we read: *And being found in appearance as a man, He humbled Himself by becoming obedient to the point of death, even death on a cross. Therefore also God highly exalted Him, and bestowed on Him the name which is above every name, that at the name of Jesus every knee should bow, of those who are in heaven, and on earth, and under the earth, and that every tongue should confess that Jesus Christ is Lord, to the glory of God the Father.*

Ephesians 1:20-21 says: *Which He brought about in Christ, when He raised Him from the dead, and seated Him at His right hand in the heavenly places, far above all rule and authority and power and dominion, and every name that is named, not only in this age, but also in the one to come.*

The name of Jesus Christ is the highest and most glorious name in all the realms of time and eternity. What a privilege is ours as

Christians to have been given the right to use His name. We now represent Christ in the earth. We bear His name. We are His ambassadors (2 Corinthians 5:20).

And these signs will accompany those who have believed: in My name they will cast out demons, . . . — *Mark 16:17*

Jesus Christ has given to us, His people, the legal right to use His name. We are His representatives in the earth and are to cast out demons as He did, to heal the sick as He did, and to preach and teach. But it is all to be done in His name.

The early church knew the power of Jesus' name. Wherever the disciples went, they preached, healed, baptized, cast out demons — all in the name of the Lord Jesus Christ.

To bear His name is not only a great privilege, but also a great responsibility. We are acting in the place of Jesus. We are speaking on His behalf. When we speak in His name, led by the Holy Spirit, it is as though Jesus Himself were speaking.

In the name of Jesus Christ we are boldly to confront the enemy. Just as Jesus is feared in the nether world, so likewise are those who come in His name.

In Acts 16 we read the account of Paul in Philippi and how for many days he was bothered by a slave girl with a spirit of divination who followed him and his companions crying out saying that they were servants of the Most High God. Finally Paul used his authority in the name of Jesus: . . . *"I command you in the name of Jesus Christ to come out of her!" And it came out at that very moment (verse 18).*

This exercising of spiritual authority resulted in Paul and Silas being cast in prison. The masters of the slave girl could no longer use her to bring profit by fortune-telling. In Jesus' name the spirit of divination had fled.

2. The Word of God

Another powerful weapon is the Word of God.

When Jesus was being tempted by Satan, He used the Scriptures to drive back the attack. He responded to each temptation by quoting from the book of Deuteronomy (Luke 4:4 and Deuteronomy 8:3; Luke 4:8 and Deuteronomy 6:13; Luke 4:12 and Deuteronomy 6:16).

If we are to use the Word of God as a weapon against the enemy, we must know what the Bible says. Jesus Himself was only able to use the Scriptures because He had familiarized Himself with them. We too must saturate our minds with the Word of God: read it; study it; memorize it.

When we have the Word of God in our minds and hearts, because we know the true facts, with authority we can make war against the enemy. We can say: "Enemy, you have no legal right to touch my life because I am redeemed by the blood of Jesus (Ephesians 1:7). Sin is not master of my life (Romans 6:14). I am freed from sin (Romans 6:7). Sickness leave my body, for by the stripes of Jesus I am healed (1 Peter 2:24)."

We can also use the Word of God to defend ourselves against enemy attacks. The enemy often attacks by putting thoughts in our minds. He may try to convince us that he is too strong for us, and there is no way we can get free from him. We can respond by saying: "Enemy, that is not true. Jesus has rendered you powerless (Hebrews 2:14). And Jesus has given me authority over all the works of the enemy (Luke 10:19)." He may try to condemn us for a certain sin even though we have confessed it and asked God's forgiveness. We can respond: "Enemy, there is no condemnation to those who are in Christ Jesus (Romans 8:1)."

When using God's Word, there is no need to quote exactly word for word from any particular Bible translation. It is the truth of what the Scripture says that is important. Often it is easiest and best to paraphrase the truths in your own words. Verses you have memorized, of course, can be quoted word for word. Whichever way you use the Word, truth is truth, and the enemy is subject to it.

Another way to use the Word, is to identify with Bible stories. We could, for example, say to the enemy: "Gideon overcame the Midianites by the sword of the Lord. And as he came against them, so we come against you. As he overcame them, so we overcome you. . . ."

As well as being able to use God's written Word, we must also learn to hear and be led by God's word as He speaks to us today through His Holy Spirit. When Jesus was on earth, He was in constant communion with His Father. He did nothing on His own initiative, but only what the Father told Him (John 8:28-29).

We must learn to be led by the Spirit in what we do, in how we pray, and in how we come against the enemy. This also applies when quoting Scriptures. We must not quote God's Word just for the sake of throwing verses at demons. We need to learn to flow in the direction the Holy Spirit gives, speaking the truths He brings to our mind.

There may be times when you are led to emphasize a certain

Bible truth and to keep on reinforcing it against the enemy. If, for example, the Holy Spirit is emphasizing the word "cleanse," cooperate with Him along this line and speak against the hidden stronghold until the burden lifts. You could say: "The Word of God declares that the blood of Jesus cleanses me. I am clean now through His Word. I release the cleansing flow of the Holy Spirit. All uncleanness is going. Every evil spirit going now. Jesus Christ is my purity. Come out in Jesus' name. Thank You, Lord, I am clean. I am clean now. Old things have passed away; all things have become new. I enforce the victory of Calvary. Be cleansed in Jesus' name."

As strongholds are uncovered, you may speak in this vein for perhaps a short period or perhaps a long period — even an hour or more. The secret is learning to flow in the Holy Spirit. This only comes through experience.

A carpenter chooses a particular tool for a particular moment. A golfer selects the right club for a particular drive. Likewise, we are to use the tool or tools appropriate for the time. Using tools for the sake of using them, is not the answer. Be selective. And if a truth or key is quickened to your heart, stay with it. The Holy Spirit will guide you in the general flow of how to speak.

The word of God also comes through gifts of the Spirit: the word of knowledge, discernings of spirits, and the word of wisdom. More will be said about these later.

3. The Blood of Jesus Christ

The blood of Jesus Christ was the price paid for our redemption:
Knowing that you were not redeemed with perishable things like silver or gold from your futile way of life inherited from your forefathers, but with precious blood, as of a lamb unblemished and spotless, the blood of Christ. — *1 Peter 1:18-19*

As the Lamb of God, and as the substitute for each one of us, Jesus Christ died the terrible death of crucifixion. He died that we might live. He became sin for us that we might know His righteousness. He took our sickness that we might have His health. He became bound that we might be set free.

The offering of Himself was accepted by the Father as a perfect sacrifice (Hebrews 10), and thus divine justice was satisfied. Man could now be released from the dominion of sin, sickness, and Satan, because the full price had been paid for his redemption.

And I heard a loud voice in heaven, saying, "Now the salvation,

and the power, and the kingdom of our God and the authority of His Christ have come, for the accuser of our brethren has been thrown down, who accuses them before our God day and night. And they overcame him because of the blood of the Lamb and because of the word of their testimony, and they did not love their life even to death."
— Revelation 12:10-11

We too overcome Satan and his hosts by the blood of the Lamb and the word of our testimony. The "word of our testimony" means we are to testify to what the Word says the blood has accomplished. Demons hate to hear this confession:

1. I am cleansed from all sin by the blood of Jesus. (1 John 1:7)
2. I am brought near to God by the blood of Christ. (Ephesians 2:13)
3. I am justified by the blood of Jesus. (Romans 5:8-9)
4. I have redemption through the blood of Jesus. (Ephesians 1:7)
5. I am sanctified through the blood of Jesus. (Hebrews 13:12)
6. I have peace with God through His blood. (Colossians 1:20)
7. I am in a covenent relationship with God through the blood of Jesus. (Mark 14:24)
8. I am purchased by the blood of Jesus. (Acts 20:28)
9. The blood of Christ cleanses my conscience. (Hebrews 9:14)
10. I have confidence to come into the presence of God by the blood of Jesus. (Hebrews 10:19-22)
11. The blood of Christ is precious to me. (1 Peter 1:19)

Use the words of your testimony to make war against the enemy: "Through the blood of Jesus Christ I have been redeemed, bought out of Satan's dominion. Through His blood I enjoy a covenant relationship with God. I stand before my Father's throne with confidence, my mind and conscience cleansed. Spirits of darkness come out now in Jesus' name. I drive you out of your hiding places. The precious blood of Jesus sanctifies me now. Lord, I praise You that right now the blood speaks release."

While staying on a sheep station in Australia, the station owners told us that one of their young daughters was continually having terrible nightmares. The mother understood how she was suffering because she had had the same kind of dreams when she was a child.

We spoke to the parents of the power of the blood of Jesus Christ and of their authority as believers to set their daughter free. Around ten o'clock, when she was sleeping soundly, we went into her bedroom, and laid our hands on her. We instructed the parents to listen carefully to the way we prayed so that if the nightmares were not broken through this one operation of faith, they could continue praying on subsequent occasions until she was completely free.

Quietly, we declared the power of the blood of Jesus Christ and that on the grounds of sacrificial blood the enemy had no legal right to afflict the child. For a few minutes, without her waking, we rebuked the source of the nightmares, praising God for the redeeming blood. Next morning she exclaimed, "Mummy, I didn't have any bad dreams last night!"

Through later contacts with the family, we were pleased to learn that she has never since been troubled with nightmares. They were broken the night we prayed. There is power in the blood of the Lamb!

4. The Holy Spirit

The Holy Spirit is the one who represents Jesus in our midst. He is the one who strengthens us for the battle, who quickens the words we utter in faith in Jesus' name.

Jesus Himself did not commence His public ministry until He was anointed with the Holy Spirit (Luke 3:21-23). After His resurrection, He commanded His disciples to wait in Jerusalem until they were filled with the Holy Spirit. They had been born again of the Spirit (John 20:22), but not baptized with the Spirit (Acts 1:8; 2:1-4).

It is necessary for us also to be filled with the Holy Spirit. Until we have commenced the Spirit-filled walk, we will never successfully and consistently deal with evil spirits.

The baptism in the Holy Spirit is not an end result in itself, but a gateway through which we enter into new realms of experiencing and serving God. As those born again of the Spirit, we are to come to Jesus Christ, the Baptizer in the Holy Spirit (Luke 3:16), and ask Him to fill us. We receive His Spirit by faith, even as we receive salvation by faith. To some, this entering the Spirit-filled walk, passing through this gateway into a daily walk in the Spirit, is a dynamic and thrilling experience. To others, it is a quiet receiving. My experience was the former, whereas Shirley's was the latter. Whatever our kind of experience, we enter into a new dimension of Christian living that is to be maintained daily by faith. Ephesians 5:18.

Jesus Christ, the Son of God, ministered in total dependence upon the Holy Spirit: *You know of Jesus of Nazareth, how God anointed Him with the Holy Spirit and with power, and how He went about doing good, and healing all who were oppressed by the devil; for God was with Him (Acts 10:38).*

The Holy Spirit is the power that enables us to cast out demons. As we speak words of faith against the enemy, the Holy Spirit enforces what we say. He makes our words as sharp arrows piercing into enemy strongholds; He makes them as heavy hammers destroying; He makes them as flaming shafts dispelling darkness.

Jesus called the Holy Spirit the "finger of God." In replying to accusations that He was casting out demons by Beelzebul the ruler of the demons, He said, *"But if I cast out demons by the finger of God, then the kingdom of God has come upon you" (Luke 11:20)*. In Matthew 12:28 where the same incident is recorded it reads: *"But if I cast out demons by the Spirit of God, then the kingdom of God has come upon you."*

Shirley and I were praying against spirits of uncleanness in a young woman and the Holy Spirit was taking our words and a flow of deliverance was being experienced. After sitting quietly for quite some time, she suddenly burst out crying. When we asked her why, she said that a spirit within her had just said mockingly that it was hiding and could not be found and was not coming out. Immediately my eyes were opened to "see" the spirit, and placing my hand on her, I said, "By the Holy Spirit's illumination I see you. You cannot hide and you are leaving right now. In Jesus' name, go!" At once the spirit reacted in fear and quickly left, and she felt an obvious release. We all rejoiced that the "finger of God," the Holy Spirit, had reached within to seek out the spirit where it was hiding and to enforce the commands we had given in Jesus' name.

5. Praise

At the Olympic Games competitors strive after medals, and those who are successful receive much praise, especially for outstanding performances. On the natural plane we honor with praise those who achieve.

On the spiritual plane we are to honor Almighty God with praise for His greatness and glory. We are to be excited with Him and to praise Him for His perfection, His works, and His benefits through the Lord Jesus Christ.

Shout joyfully to the Lord, all the earth.
Serve the Lord with gladness;
Come before Him with joyful singing. . . .
Enter His gates with thanksgiving,
And His courts with praise.
Give thanks to Him; bless His name.   *— Psalm 100:1-2, 4*

Praise is a powerful weapon over Satan's works. For years I knew the importance of praising God, but was so inwardly bound that I found it extremely hard. Within my heart I could do it a little, but outwardly, it was very difficult.

For years I asked and asked God for release in my life, but it never came. It was not until I received the provisions by faith and — difficult though it was — began to praise God for the victory, that the desires of my heart and the requests of countless petitions began to become my experience.

Because the enemy knows there is power in audible praise, he does all he can to resist it. Amazingly, all he has to do to stop some people praising, is make them feel like not doing it. Let us not give in so easily to the enemy. Whether we feel like it or not, we are to make every possible effort to praise God.

Through Him then, let us continually offer up a sacrifice of praise to God, that is, the fruit of lips that give thanks to His name.
— Hebrews 13:15

Paul and Silas knew the power of praise. At Philippi they were severely beaten, thrown into prison, and their feet put in stocks. *But about midnight Paul and Silas were praying and singing hymns of praise to God, . . . and suddenly there came a great earthquake, . . . and immediately all the doors were opened, and everyone's chains were unfastened (Acts 16:25-26).* It pleased the Lord to bring great deliverance as they prayed and praised.

2 Chronicles 20:1-30 tells the predicament of Jehoshaphat and the people of Judah who were about to be attacked by the Moabites, the Ammonites, and the Meunites. While they sought the Lord in prayer and fasting, the Holy Spirit came upon Jahaziel and through him directed the people to go forward the next day against the enemy and promised them that God would bring a great deliverance. With the word of victory in their hearts, the people worshipped and praised God. The next day they went towards the enemy led by the musicians and singers. As they began to sing praises to God, the invading armies were thrown into a panic and began fighting each other. By the time the Judean army arrived on the scene, all the enemy lay dead on the ground. Not one person had escaped.

When battling unseen spirits, it is important that we mingle our commands with praise to God. There are times when we should major on praise. Sometimes when praying for people, I meet spirits that are very stubborn, and no matter what other weapons are used, they seem of no avail. At such times, I often feel led to declare that the victory is ours and to concentrate on praising God for it. We have seen some significant releases in the midst of continuing praise when nothing else would work. God inhabits the praises of His people (Psalm 22:3).

One evening while ministering in Papua New Guinea, we were privileged to see the Holy Spirit come upon a gathering of young nationals in a great wave of deliverance. The Word had been preached and God had touched a number of lives. While thinking to myself that after another ten minutes I would conclude the meeting, I encouraged everyone to praise the Lord. Two lads on my right then began to praise God with such enthusiasm that it brought a sudden quickening in my spirit. I sensed something was about to happen. The enthusiasm spread like a fire and the presence of God became very real. In the midst of this "high praise," with many leaping for joy, great deliverance began to take place. Demons were leaving with loud cries. The atmosphere was full of the cries of terror of demons and the shouts of victory of God's people. Although many times we have witnessed similar manifestations, this night was different in that there was an intense awareness of God's Spirit. The wave of deliverance continued for about twenty minutes.

When we concluded the meeting, I suggested that those who were still battling with unbroken demonic pressures, remain behind. Twenty or so stayed and counselors began to pray for them individually. After a few minutes, the Holy Spirit fell again with the same intensity. This time the demon manifestations were extremely violent. Heads were banging on the concrete floor, and other such things were happening. We ran from person to person commanding release in Jesus' name. What a night of victory!

This intense move of God was begun by Christians wholeheartedly, spontaneously, and intensely praising God. Increasingly, we shall witness great signs, wonders, and miracles, not just in a one-to-one ministry in a healing line, but in a whole congregation as the Holy Spirit is released in power through our faith and our genuine praise.

6. Speaking in Tongues

On the day of Pentecost when the disciples were filled with the Holy Spirit, those gathered nearby heard them, in their own tongues, speaking of God's mighty deeds (Acts 2:11).

Paul knew the blessing of this unlearned language of the Spirit. While giving instruction on its use in the church, he said, *"I thank God, I speak in tongues more than you all" (1 Corinthians 14:18).* Paul communicated with God continually by speaking in tongues. He was aware that in so doing, his own spirit was experiencing direct communication with the Lord, and he was edifying himself in the process. 1 Corinthians 14:1-4.

Although some people commence speaking in tongues with great ease when they are filled with the Holy Spirit, this was not my experience. I had had a dynamic infilling that had made me as it were "drunk" in the Spirit, but at the time I did not speak in tongues. It was not until twelve months later, when a patient missionary stayed with me and prayed me through, that I came into a glorious release. This was a milestone in my Christian experience. Looking back now, I can see why I had such a battle. The demons within me had been resisting the releasing of this supernatural ability. They knew what a strength it would be to me.

Over the long days of my searching, struggling, and suffering, the ability to speak in tongues was a lifesaver. I don't know how I could have continued on without the release this gift gave me. It was the only way through which I could express the deep cries of my heart to God. Through it I was edified and strengthened.

Before being able to speak in tongues, I was often frustrated at my inability to freely express praise to the Lord. The frustration ended when the gift was released. Speaking in tongues also makes a way to pray more freely. When one is lost for understanding on how to pray, praying in the Spirit is invaluable.

There was a time when for months I had been battling in my mind to keep right attitudes to two people. Whenever I met them or thought of them, thoughts of resentment rose within me. Not being one to harbor resentment or unforgiveness, I couldn't understand what was happening. Continually I confessed these increasing thoughts as sin, becoming very weary of it. No one — not even the two men — had any indication how I felt because I was choosing to live in obedience to God's Word and love them.

In the midst of these days, I began to pray and fast. On the third day as I was praising God, something manifested in my mind saying, "My name is hate. My name is hate." This caught me unawares. Then I realized that behind my wrong attitudes were spirits of hatred that were manifesting. I hadn't wanted to hate. Something within me, that wasn't me, had been trying to make me cooperate with its own vile nature.

Because at that time I didn't know the way to get free, all I could do was seek God and pray in tongues, knowing that in so doing I was

77

praying in the will of God. The following morning I knelt by the bed between the hours of ten and eleven, uplifting this need to the Lord, and praying in tongues. After the hour, although nothing outward had happened, I sensed I was free. This proved to be so. Three days later I met one of the men in the street and greeted him in my usual way. To my delight, instead of resentment rising up in me, I felt a beautiful flow of love. I was free!

The Lord later showed me how these spirits had come in during my childhood, and how they had lain low since my conversion waiting for a time to rear their ugly heads.

As well as praising and praying in tongues, I have discovered that we can also *command in tongues*. When praying for others, often I am led by the Holy Spirit to speak to demons in tongues, and I have seen clear evidences of blessing as a result. There are times when the weapon or key is not declaring what the Blood has done, nor quoting the Word, nor using the name of Jesus (although this may be done in the language being spoken), but simply to speak in tongues. Demons know what we are saying. Usually I find a tremendous authority within me as I do so. Although normally I do not understand what I am saying, I am aware that direct commands and declarations are being made by the Holy Spirit. Usually I find I speak in a language different from what I use mostly in personal devotion and praise.

A young man came for counsel, and when I looked to the Lord for direction, I was led to command in tongues. Within me I became aware that we were touching a deep, hidden area of bondage, and although no demons were leaving him, I sensed that a weakening of the hold was taking place. The young man was cooperating with me and inwardly standing against the enemy. The commands and declarations in tongues continued to flow for thirty minutes while my strength in no way abated. During all this time the man felt nothing inwardly happening, but sat quietly on a chair.

Suddenly, without warning, he — or should I say the demons — let out a loud cry and threw him forward onto the floor. The moment the spirits manifested, the Lord showed me the name of the stronghold: homosexuality. I later learned that he had been involved in this sin fifteen years before, when he was still unconverted. For two more hours we battled in the midst of demonic manifestations.

By speaking in tongues under the direction of the Holy Spirit, these long-hidden demons had been revealed and weakened, and now were being cleansed from his personality. There is a time to command in tongues.

7. Binding and Loosing

And if I by Beelzebul cast out demons, by whom do your sons cast them out? Consequently they shall be your judges. But if I cast out demons by the Spirit of God, then the kingdom of God has come upon you. Or how can anyone enter the strong man's house and carry off his property, unless he first binds the strong man? And then he will plunder his house.
— *Matthew 12:27-29*

Sometimes the key or weapon to use is binding the enemy. In the last incident mentioned in the previous section, when I spoke in tongues for thirty minutes, I knew I was binding the enemy, and in so doing, weakening him. When this key is quickened to you, you must believe that what you say is happening. Use your imagination and see yourself wrapping and tying the enemy with every statement:

"You works of darkness, we use our authority over you. In Jesus Christ's name, we bind you. We render you inoperative. We tie you so tightly that you are restricted from ever working again. You are becoming weaker and weaker. You are defeated through the death and resurrection of Jesus Christ. He it is who has the keys of death and hell. We represent Him. We are strong in Him. Be bound, totally bound in Jesus' name. Thank You Lord, the enemy is becoming weaker and weaker. He cannot resist our commands, for we are triumphant in Christ. You are bound. You hidden spirits, you are bound. Release this child of God now in Jesus' name."

When I pray, I get totally involved, because it's not just a matter of saying the right words, but a conscious, willing cooperation with the Holy Spirit that at times can be very demanding. Sometimes I stand as I speak; or kneel, or walk around. Often I use gestures, for we are binding, speaking to, and dealing with real, intelligent, spirit identities.

In a higher sense, Satan was "bound" through his being disarmed at Christ's resurrection (Colossians 2:15).

Since then the children share in flesh and blood, He Himself likewise also partook of the same, that through death He might render powerless him who had the power of death, that is, the devil.
— *Hebrews 2:14*

In Christ, it is God's purpose to "render powerless" or "reduce to inactivity" (Greek: *katargeo*) the devil and his agents.

Satan's head has been bruised (Genesis 3:15); he has suffered an overwhelming blow by the mighty Deliverer; yet in his disarmed state, he still tries to deceive and destroy the sons of men. There will come a day when he will be put down forever; but until that day comes, the church must stand up to him, declaring his defeat and enforcing Christ's victory.

Matthew 18:18-20 also speaks of binding and loosing in the name of Jesus Christ:

Truly I say to you, whatever you shall bind on earth shall be bound in heaven; and whatever you loose on earth shall be loosed in heaven. Again I say to you, that if two of you agree on earth about anything that they may ask, it shall be done for them by My Father who is in heaven. For where two or three have gathered together in My name, there I am in their midst.

As we agree or harmonize together (not merely mentally agreeing, but harmonizing because we are being led by the Spirit of God), we can declare the binding of the enemy's power and the loosing of God's saints. The Holy Spirit can place on our hearts how we are to pray and what we are to say. We are not trying to bring to pass our plans, but working together with God to release His plans and purposes.

When I pray for someone to be set free, I usually begin my commands to the enemy by saying: "We bind your activity within this life in Jesus' name." Sometimes I say it only once; other times I spend quite some time declaring a "binding" on the hidden spirits.

Psalm 149 shows the authority that the saints of God have in dealing with spiritual powers. We are *to bind their kings with chains, and their nobles with fetters of iron (verse 8).* Hallelujah!

8. Confession of Identification

I used to read Romans 6 many times, but it was a frustration to me. What it said did not match my experience. It said that I was free from sin, but I knew that I wasn't. What was wrong? Why didn't it work? Was God's Word not true? — that was impossible. Eventually I came to see that instead of questioning God's Word, I was to accept it, and confess it. When I first did this, I felt I was confessing to a lie. But realizing that God's Word was not a lie, I continued to confess it. Gradually faith rose in my heart, and the truth of God's Word began to become a reality in my experience.

The whole of Romans 6 needs to be read and meditated upon often. Our victory over Satan is actually Christ's victory in which we share. When by revelation (and it is only by revelation) we understand these truths, we can hold fast a faith confession that is extremely powerful. Even if we don't fully understand the truths, we can still confess them, for they are truth. Through our confession the Holy Spirit can cause us to come into understanding.

Romans 6 says that when Jesus died on the cross, we died with Him. Our sinful adamic nature was put to death when Jesus was put to death. When He was buried, we were buried with Him. When He was raised from the dead, we also were raised with Him in newness of life. 2 Corinthians 5:17 says: *If any man is in Christ, he is a new creature; the old things passed away; behold, new things have come.*

By identifying with Jesus Christ in death, we have elected to die to the power and corruption of sin; to die to ourselves, our self-centeredness, our rebellion, our plans, our pride, our reputation, etc. We have chosen to be free from sin and self.

By identifying in burial, we are saying: "I am dead and out of sight as far as this world is concerned. Because I am dead, sin has no power over me. Because I am dead and buried, Satan, the god of this world, cannot touch me; he cannot influence me; for through death I have been released from the power of sin and Satan."

But our confession does not end there. We go on to confess that we have been raised in newness of life with Christ. The old is behind: the new has come. We stand in righteousness, in freedom, in boldness; as conquerors, as children of God, with our heads held high. Sin has no dominion over us. Sickness has no power over us. Satan cannot touch us, for we are in Christ.

If we have been greatly rejected in our life, and spirits of rejection have found a place and are continually stirring within, one of the keys to release is to say repeatedly what we have become in Christ:

"Spirits of rejection, I bind you in Jesus' name. You have no legal right to continue to afflict me; for I am identified with Jesus Christ, my Savior and Deliverer. When Jesus died at Calvary, I died in Him. Through death and burial I have died to this world; I have died to your domination; I have died to the feelings of emotion and hurt you bring. Rejection, through death your power is broken. I am now alive in Christ. His power has set me free. His love fills my innermost parts. I am healed. I am whole. And, Lord Jesus, I thank You for my identification with You. I have died and I have risen. Rejection has no place in me, no power over me; for I am no longer in Adam, but I am in Christ. Thank You, Lord Jesus, that these spirits are leaving me — right now. Your Holy Spirit is weakening their hold — right now. This stronghold is crumbling — right now. With every natural breath spirits of darkness are leaving me. Every band is broken. The love of God fills me. I am set free."

This truth of identification is of utmost importance. We will not be able to rise up out of every satanic bondage, unless we have an increasing reliance upon, and identification with, Jesus Christ in death and resurrection.

9. Fasting

In the New Testament there is no specific command to fast; however there are passages in which it is taken for granted that Christians would fast:

Then the disciples of John came to Him, saying, "Why do we and the Pharisees fast, but Your disciples do not fast?" And Jesus said to them, "The attendants of the bridegroom cannot mourn as long as the bridegroom is with them, can they? But the days will come when the bridegroom is taken away from them, and then they will fast.

— Matthew 9:14-15.

In Matthew 6:16-18 Jesus, again indicating that His disciples would fast, exhorts them to have their motives pure: *And whenever you fast, do not put on a gloomy face as the hypocrites do, for they neglect their appearance in order to be seen fasting by men. Truly I say to you, they have their reward in full. But you, when you fast, anoint your head, and wash your face so that you may not be seen fasting by men, but by your Father who is in secret; and your Father who sees in secret will repay you.*

Fasting must be mixed with faith. During the difficult years before I began to find release, I constantly resorted to prayer and fasting. Fasting was the only way I knew to lift the intensity of the bouts of depression that weighed upon me. It would take a few days to significantly lift the pressure. Looking back, I realize now that although the Lord honored my seeking Him in this way, I mixed very little faith with my fasting. It is by faith we overcome — not just fasting. My cry had been, "Lord, do something. Help! Please change me." I was putting the initiative on the Lord, expecting Him to do something; but the initiative needed to be on me. I did not know I was to set myself free.

Sometimes a period of fasting (whether short or long) can greatly assist in breaking strongholds. A dimension of power is released when a person fasts with the right motivation and with faith. Occasionally when counseling, I say to someone, "When you have fasted for a day (three days, or perhaps a week), then with the ground more prepared for battle, we will pray for deliverance." Every so often, there is a strength and resistance of the enemy that needs to be weakened through prayer and fasting.

There was an occasion when the disciples were unable to cast out a demon, and Jesus had to come to their assistance. When they asked why they could not cast it out, Jesus replied, . . . *"This kind can come forth by nothing, but by prayer and fasting" (Mark 9:29 AV).*

Isaiah 58 speaks of right and wrong fasting. Verse 6 says: *Is this not the fast which I chose, To loosen the bonds of wickedness, To undo the bands of the yoke, And to let the oppressed go free, And break every yoke?*

10. The Laying On of Hands

Jesus laid hands on people, and He said believers were to do the same (Luke 4:40-41; Mark 16:17-18).

An impartation of the Holy Spirit is released through clean vessels as in faith hands are laid upon the person needing deliverance.

Demons in people often react loudly and violently when hands are laid on, and will try to push the hands away. They know well the impartation that comes, and they want no part of it.

In a personal counseling situation, I extend my hands most of the time when I am commanding. It is not necessary, however, to lay hands on a person when praying for deliverance. In public deliverance meetings, I have seen many people set free with no one laying hands on them. If you are in need of deliverance, it is not a necessity that you seek out someone to lay hands on you and pray.

The laying on of hands is not a mere form to go through. You must be informed of its significance, and realize what is happening in the unseen realm. When you are aware of this, you will take every opportunity to impart the Holy Spirit in this way.

Sometimes people comment that they feel heat or fire flowing through my hands as I pray for them. Personally, I have never felt anything, but I do have an awareness in my spirit of what God is doing. When ministering, do not be bound by natural feelings. We minister, not on a natural plane, but on a spiritual plane.

A word of warning: The laying on of hands is a spiritual exercise which can be used for both good and evil. It is possible to receive an impartation which is not from the Holy Spirit. We need to be selective as to whom we let pray for us. Unfortunately, there are people who are not right with God. Some are puffed up with pride, wanting to be in the limelight, thinking they have a ministry which they do not have. All believers should be in a place where they can lay hands on another and impart blessing; but sad to say, this is not so.

On the other hand, I encourage Christians who are not fully free to lay hands on others and pray for them. If a Christian is honestly walking in the light, and pressing through to more and more release, and is humble of heart, and loves people, and desires to impart a blessing; then he can impart blessing through the laying on of hands. People like this, God will use. He does not wait until we are perfect. We may be sick, and yet God will heal through us. Fear may still grip us to a measure, and yet the Lord will use us to cast spirits of fear out of others and minister a new level of peace to them, even though we are imperfect vessels.

Don't wait until you are completely free to heal or deliver others. Just have your heart right. Be humble and dependent upon the Lord Jesus. Pray in faith. Command in faith. Impart in faith. Sometimes the Lord will bless and heal you while you are ministering to others. We impart by faith; we receive by faith. Our feelings do not tell us we are imparting or receiving — our faith does.

Regarding where to lay hands: Hands can be laid on the head or elsewhere. When praying for men, I like to place my hands on the stomach area because the deepest releases come from this region. Sitting to the side or behind the person makes this easy. However, I never lay my hands on the stomach of a woman or touch any area of her flesh. One must be extremely wise when praying for members of the opposite sex, and must give no ground for any appearance of evil. When I pray for women, whenever possible, I have a woman counselor with me. Men ministering to men and women to women affords no problems.

11. Anointed Music

The world would be a poorer place if there were no music in it — and the church likewise. The Holy Spirit will anoint music that He inspires, and thus another channel is opened through which to receive refreshment in the midst of spiritual battles.

When the kings of Israel, Judah, and Edom sought Elisha for counsel, the Lord gave Elisha a plan of war to defeat the Moabites. It came in the midst of music. Elisha had requested that a minstrel be brought, and it was as the minstrel played that the power of the Lord came on Elisha (1 Kings 3:15).

Again we see the power of anointed music in the story of David playing his harp whenever Saul was tormented by the evil spirit. His music refreshed Saul and drove away the evil spirit (1 Samuel 16:23).

To set a tone for your household, select good Christian recordings that you can have playing in your home. There are many good albums to choose from. But be selective. Some music will not bring an anointing of the Holy Spirit, but will actually release demonic activity.

When you are in the Lord's presence breaking areas of bondage in your own life, there may be times when you will find it strengthening to have music playing quietly in the background.

Songs paraphrasing Bible truths are particularly valuable in our fight against the enemy. Through songs, we can be confessing with our lips our identification with Christ, the power of the Blood, our victory in Christ, and so on.

Shirley is a songwriter and majors on putting Scripture verses and spiritual principles to music. "I'm Coming Into Resurrection Life" is a song of victory, as the following words declare:

> I'm coming into resurrection life,
> For the Lord has set me free from inward strife,
> Rise up, rise up my soul and take your victory,
> Standing on the promise that you're free,
> I'm coming out of bondage and defeat,
> A soldier in the army of the King of Kings,
> Walking in victory!
> Claiming my liberty!
> I'm coming into resurrection life.

© 1984 Shirley M. Powell.

I have personally sung this song many times. Often I have felt a victorious soldier, while on other occasions I have not. Regardless of my feelings, I sing and confess such truths daily. My faith confession releases God to establish the reality of these truths more and more in my experience.

12. Discernings of Spirits

Of the nine gifts or manifestations of the Spirit mentioned in 1 Corinthians 12, one in particular is most useful in dealing with evil spirits. It is the gift of discernings of spirits (verse 10). Jesus Christ has not left us to deal with an unseen enemy without a gift suited to this area. By the gift of discernings of spirits, one's eyes are opened to see (or perceive) things in the unseen realm that could not be perceived by natural sight or knowledge.

Any believer may on occasions operate in spiritual discernment. Indeed we are encouraged to practice it so as to mature as Christians: *Solid food is for the mature, who because of practice have their senses trained to discern good and evil (Hebrews 5:14).* However, there is a gift that is given, not to everyone, but distributed as the Spirit wills (1 Corinthians 12:11). If we find discernment operating regularly in our lives, then we can say that we have this spiritual gift. The source of the revelation is the Lord Jesus, and to Him must go the glory.

Recently, I answered a call to help a Christian young man who had had a breakdown. He came from an evangelical stream that didn't believe Christians could be demonized. Their beliefs restricted them from being able to help him. He was depressed and despairing, thinking he had lost his salvation and was damned forever. I prayed with him, rebuking the enemy as the Holy Spirit directed. After praying only thirty minutes, although he felt no manifestations, his depression greatly lifted, and his assurance of salvation returned. That night, for the first time in months, he slept soundly without medication. Three days later he was discharged from hospital. When I went to pray for him again, he told me that he had often wondered if demons were the cause of his problems, and wondered if there could possibly be one person in the world who operated in discernment and could tell him if this were so. I assured him that I personally knew numerous people who had received this gift and were using it to minister to the Body of Christ.

The gift of discernings of spirits is not restricted to discerning demons. It is also used to discern what the Holy Spirit is doing, to discern the human spirit, and to discern the presence of angels. John the Baptist discerned the Holy Spirit coming down upon Jesus in the form of a dove (Matthew 3:16). Jesus discerned that Nathanael's spirit had no falsehood (John 1:47). Elisha discerned the presence of angels (2 Kings 6:15-17).

While counseling a man who had much resentment and bitterness, I stressed the importance of forgiveness, and the need to repent. Going through the outward motions, he named people and situations and "repented," claiming forgiveness. When we began to pray against the spirits behind the scenes, I discerned that he had been dishonest and had not truly repented. I said, "Do you still have unforgiveness in your heart?" He said he did not. Again we went to prayer, but I knew he had not told the truth. A second and a third time I asked him the same question, and he gave the same response. But because I "knew" by the Holy Spirit, I turned confidently to him and said, "You have not forgiven these people. You are lying. I have a word from the Lord for you. It is repent!"

Upon being confronted, he admitted he had not, and would not, forgive. Angrily, he stormed from my office and never returned to the church again. Within a few weeks he was in jail. The last I heard of him, he was in a mental institution receiving psychiatric treatment. The more light we have, the more accountable we are. This man was shown light and given opportunity to repent, but he turned from that light and brought great judgment on himself.

Spiritual gifts, especially the discernings of spirits and the word of knowledge, enable counselors to get quickly to the root of problems. Thus much time is saved.

Some months ago a man addicted to smoking was saved, but instead of giving it up, he was soon smoking twice as much. When he shared his need and asked for prayer, I discerned spirits of failure and the fear of failure, and sensed they were the root cause of his habit. He confessed he had always felt a failure and spoken "big talk" to try to impress people. I prayed, commanding a breaking of these inward holds, until I was led to cease, which was after more than an hour. Some time later, he came to me with a puzzled look and said, "I can't understand it. You didn't pray about my smoking, but I am free." I explained that by revelation of the Holy Spirit we had dealt with the foundation that gave nicotine its place.

A young woman recently came for prayer. She had been on the mission field, but had had to leave because of a breakdown. Her concern was a physical problem, but again the Lord wanted to go deeper. I discerned a strong inner demonic hold of self-hatred that had turned her against herself, causing her not to love or think well of herself. She admitted this was the major problem in her life, and we began to command the demons to go. After only one session of deliverance, she noticed deep changes in her personality and was thrilled at the prospect of becoming a new person.

Through the gift of discernings of spirits, we can know much more about evil spirits than just perceiving their presence. We can know their names; know the strength of the bondage area; see their resistance; see their reactions and weakenings as they are bound and commanded to go; see them leaving a person; know whether holds are completely broken or partially broken; know other spirits that are closely associated with those you are dealing with; know if the counselee is doing his part to cooperate; know the level of faith the person has; and so on. It is not necessary to have any outward physical reactions to guide you. Discernment is a knowing — a perceiving — by the Holy Spirit.

The gift of discernings of spirits may operate differently through different people. Several people may be together who each operate in this gift, but with varying types or levels of insight.

Discernings of spirits is closely related to the word of knowledge and the word of wisdom. These are all revelation gifts.

While the gift of discernings of spirits gives insight to "see" the work of the enemy, the word of knowledge gives understanding as to when the problem occurred, what caused it, etc. When praying for someone, I discerned spirits of rejection, and then through a word of knowledge knew that their hold had been strengthened when the person was a teenager and had nearly drowned. I was also able to tell the time, place, and circumstances surrounding the incident. Such manifestations of God's Spirit show the counselee God's personal concern and love, and help activate his faith to receive release.

How the church needs all the gifts of the Spirit operating in their full measure. As Western Christians, we are often too "clever," too "educated," too "self-reliant," and not child-like enough in dependence and faith. Even many Pentecostal and Charismatic churches have been infiltrated with terms and methods of modern psychology, and have rejected the Holy Spirit's wisdom and power.

Remember: spiritual bondages are broken with spiritual weapons. *The weapons of our warfare are not of the flesh, but divinely powerful for the destruction of fortresses (2 Corinthians 10:4).*

All believers, especially those with leadership and counseling responsibilities, should be earnestly desiring spiritual gifts (1 Corinthians 14:1).

Chapter 8

The Key of Faith

There are two worlds. One is the material world which is seen, but temporal. The other is the spiritual world which is unseen, but eternal.

Just as we entered the reality of the temporal world by a physical birth, so too we enter the reality of the spiritual world of the kingdom of God by a spiritual birth.

Jesus said, . . . *"Unless one is born again, he cannot see the kingdom of God" (John 3:3)*. Also He said, *"That which is born of the flesh is flesh, and that which is born of the Spirit is spirit" (John 3:6)*. When a person comes to Jesus Christ in repentance and faith, yielding himself to the lordship of Jesus Christ, an inward miracle takes place. The Holy Spirit imparts new life, making the person's spirit alive to God. He becomes a member of the family of God, and receives the gift of eternal life. He is given access to the presence of God, and commences a relationship with God.

This new birth takes place through a faith action. Faith is imparted to us in order for us to come into God's kingdom. *By grace you have been saved through faith . . . (Ephesians 2:8)*. The faith imparted to us is a measure of faith. It has to grow to enable us to appreciate more and more the Lord Himself and the power of His kingdom.

Before the new birth, we are bound to the material world to which we relate through our senses: seeing, feeling, tasting, hearing, and smelling. We walk by "sight" knowledge, not by "revelation" knowledge. After the new birth, revelation knowledge comes to us as the Holy Spirit enlightens God's Word. Thus the unseen kingdom becomes a reality to us. The faculties of our spirit begin to see (or perceive) this new realm. We begin to walk by "faith." We are saved by faith, and we walk by faith.

Defining Faith

Now faith is the assurance [AV: substance] of things hoped for, the conviction [AV: evidence] of things not seen. — *Hebrews 11:1*

In the Amplified New Testament this verse reads: *Now faith is the assurance (the confirmation, the title-deed) of the things [we] hope for, being the proof of things [we] do not see and the conviction of their reality — faith perceiving as real fact what is not revealed to the senses.*

The words *faith* and *believe* come from the same Greek root. The word for "faith" is *pistis*, a noun; for "believe" it is *pisteuo*, a verb. We can therefore say that exercising faith is believing, and believing is exercising faith. A believer is one who has faith. He who has faith is a believer. Simply stated: a believer is one who trusts God's Word.

Through faith we can partake of the provisions of God's kingdom. In relation to receiving these provisions —

FAITH IS: — the **action** of stepping out on the Word of God.

— the **power** that brings the promise of God into tangible possession.

— the **assurance** that that hoped for is now yours.

— the **conviction** that the unseen provision is your present possession.

— the **confession** of thankfulness for the fulfilled promise.

Hope says: "I *will* receive."

Faith says: "I *have* received."

The Call to Walk by Faith

For we walk by faith, not by sight. — *2 Corinthians 5:7*

Now that no one is justified by the Law before God is evident; for, "The righteous man shall live by faith." — *Galatians 3:11*

I have been crucified with Christ; and it is no longer I who live, but Christ lives in me; and the life which I now live in the flesh I live by faith in the Son of God, who loved me, and delivered Himself up for me. — *Galatians 2:20*

You and I are called to walk by faith. Our Christian walk began with a faith surrender to Jesus Christ. Everything we receive from God is by the currency of faith. Forgiveness, healing, deliverance, guidance, protection, etc., are all received by faith.

All your life, you have communicated with the temporal world through your senses. Perhaps now, having come to Christ, you are trying to relate to the spiritual world with your senses. It won't work! Your senses must come under the domination of your spirit. Your spirit, from where faith flows, is to have the upper hand. You must start to walk in the light of revelation knowledge — truth that has come through God's Word. It is your spirit that relates to the Word and to God's kingdom, not your senses.

Pleasing God Through Faith

By faith Enoch was taken up so that he should not see death; and he was not found because God took him up; for he obtained the witness that before his being taken up he was pleasing to God. And without faith it is impossible to please Him, for he who comes to God must believe that He is, and that He is a rewarder of those who seek Him.
— Hebrews 11:5-6

Enoch walked with God and pleased God. Why? Because of his faith. Do you want to please God? Then you must walk by the Word of God. How strong are these words: . . . *Without faith it is impossible to please Him*. . . . It is impossible!

For years I prayed and prayed, asking, asking, asking for the Lord to change me, to set me free. I prayed hours every day, read the Word constantly, memorized hundreds of Bible verses, fasted often; but I was not set free. If anyone was desperate, I was. I did all in my power to release God's hand. I visited churches and went out on altar calls, but was never touched. It always seemed to be someone else who got blessed; yet I was sure I sought God as fervently as anyone.

Time and time again I would cry: "Lord, You say in Your Word that if we seek You with all the heart we will find You. What is all the heart? How can I do more than I'm doing?"

Finally, after I had spent a full year in prayer and fastings, I came to a place where I felt I had run out of the ability to keep seeking, to keep striving. I was spiritually and physically exhausted. I was at the end of myself.

In this place of weakness, the Lord brought two things to my attention: First, the work of Jesus at Calvary — a perfect sacrifice for a full redemption. God had already done His part to provide my deliverance. Second, the key of faith. I was now to do my part and receive by faith Calvary's provision. I said, "Lord, I am a dead man. I have died to this world and to my own ability and strength." The Holy

91

Spirit whispered to my heart, "Rise up." I said, "How, Lord?" And He simply said, "By faith."

The words *by faith* rang in my heart, and I began to search the Scriptures. My eyes were opened to see how I could exercise faith, and as I began to believe, the turning point came. I commenced the pathway of release. Slowly I began to rise up from depression and despair. The key of faith was turning the lock. The door was opening. I was pleasing God through faith.

We can pray and plead all we like, but unless we do it God's way, we will remain in need. God's way is by faith!

The Power of Faith

Faith is so powerful that it is unlimited in its possibilities.

When the disciples expressed concern about the difficulty of a rich man entering the kingdom of God, Jesus replied, . . . *"With men this is impossible, but with God all things are possible" (Matthew 19:26).*

In Mark 9:17-29 we read of the disciples being unable to cast a spirit out of an epileptic boy who was deaf and dumb. The father had to bring the boy to Jesus, and when Jesus heard what had happened, He said, . . . *"O unbelieving generation . . . How long shall I put up with You?"* . . . He was frustrated by their lack of faith. The spirit then threw the boy into convulsions and the father implored Jesus, . . . *"If You can do anything, take pity on us and help us!"* Jesus replied, . . . *"All things are possible to him who believes."*

In Matthew 19:26 Jesus said that *with God* all things are possible. Now He says that *to him who believes* all things are possible. This means that there are unlimited possibilities to those who have faith through the Word of God.

Because faith releases such power, we need to be careful that we are using it in the right way. Some believers use it primarily for their betterment in the material realm: more of this, more of that; bigger this, bigger that. Using our faith to release material and financial benefits is not wrong, but being over-occupied with this, and thinking that God's blessings are equated only with "things," is a wrong emphasis. In this book we are relating faith to releasing God's blessings for spirit, soul, and body. The Word leaves us in no doubt that it is God's will for us to walk in liberty and health.

The Source of Faith

Faith comes through the Word of God: *So faith comes from hearing, and hearing by the word of Christ (Romans 10:17).*

If we are to receive faith, we must be hearing the Word of God. We are not to ask for faith. There is no use praying, "Lord, I have no faith. Please give me some." If we want faith to come, we must read and meditate on the Scriptures. It is not that reading Bible passages (the *logos*) alone will bring faith; we must have our heart in the Word and upon the Lord. Then the Holy Spirit will be able to take portions of the *logos*, the written Word, and quicken them to our spirit. As they are made alive to us — become the *rhema* to us — faith is released.

Stop asking for faith, and instead be before God in His Word. Select passages that speak on faith; read passages that tell what you have become in Christ. Don't struggle with your mind to try to understand, but have an open mind. As the weeks and months go by, the Word will do its own work in you, and the Teacher, the Holy Spirit, will impart to you. On a daily basis you may not see that your faith is growing, but over the weeks and months and years, you will certainly notice the difference. It is like a seed that when planted grows, matures, and is finally harvested, although the growth may not be noticed in the short term. Mark 4:26-29.

The Measure of Faith

Every Christian has a measure of faith: . . . *God has allotted to each a measure of faith (Romans 12:3).*

The measure varies from person to person, but each person's measure is to be growing. Paul told the Thessalonians that their faith had greatly grown (2 Thessalonians 1:3).

You are not to compare your faith with that of others, or to be jealous of someone else's faith, but you are to use the measure you have. You will discover that, through use, your measure increases.

As you learn to release your measure of faith, you will be encouraged by the results. At last you will discover that the Lord is working with you — no longer far away or seemingly uncaring, but He is with you. Needs are being met. You will be excited — even though there may be trying battles. Start thanking Him that you have a measure of faith.

Faith Relates to the Unseen

Faith is . . . the conviction [AV: evidence] of things not seen.
— *Hebrews 11:1*

Evidence proves the existence of something. It is impossible to have evidence for something that does not exist. In spiritual things, faith is our evidence.

The natural eye does not see the kingdom of God with its vast resources made available to us through Calvary. Ephesians 1:3 says that God . . . *has blessed us with every spiritual blessing in the heavenly places in Christ.*

Just because we don't see this realm or see its provision, doesn't mean that it doesn't exist. In fact, the unseen realm is more real than the seen, in the sense that it is eternal. Our world had a beginning and will have an end. The unseen realm is eternal, and into this realm we reach by faith.

If I were to hold a coin in my open hand and say to a group of people, "Look, in my hand is a coin," because they see the coin, they do not need faith to accept what I say. But if I put the coin behind my back and say, "In my hand is a coin," they must decide whether or not to accept my word. Because they cannot see it, they must choose to believe or to disbelieve. Their decision will be based on their trust in my word. Their not being able to see the coin does not prove it is not there. It *is* there, but to know this, they must believe my word.

In the vast unseen world, provisions for every need have been made available through Jesus Christ. The Word of God tells us this. We must choose to believe or to disbelieve God's Word. Because we do not see these provisions, does not mean they do not exist. They are real, and they are to be laid hold of. Our faith is the evidence of their existence — of their reality. Faith is the evidence of things not seen. God's Word is truth. God does not lie. He cannot lie (Titus 1:2). His Word is to be trusted. Faith comes through His Word.

2 Kings 6 tells the story of the king of Syria sending a large army with horses and chariots to capture Elisha, the prophet. The army came by night and surrounded the city. Early in the morning, Elisha's servant arose and was alarmed by what he saw. Elisha, however, was not perturbed because he not only saw the natural plane, but he had insight into the spiritual dimension. He said to his servants, *"Do not fear, for those who are with us are more than those who are with them."* Then Elisha prayed and said, *"O Lord, I pray, open his eyes that he may see"* . . . *(verses 16-17).* A strange prayer? No. Elisha

was praying that his servant might have spiritual sight. There was another world unseen to him. A real world! Just because the servant couldn't see it, didn't mean it wasn't there. It was there, but until his spiritual eyes were opened, he couldn't see. *And the Lord opened the servant's eyes, and he saw; and behold, the mountain was full of horses and chariots of fire all around Elisha" (verse 17).*

Elisha was a man of faith. His faith related to the unseen world. His faith pleased God and brought angelic deliverance.

Faith the Channel for Receiving

Now faith is the assurance of things hoped for . . .
— Hebrews 11:1

Faith is the channel through which we receive what we are hoping for. Hope and faith work together; but it is through faith that we receive the promises of God — not through hope. Many Christians think they have faith, when they only have hope.

Hope relates to the future. Faith relates to the present. Hope says, "I will be delivered." Faith says, "I am delivered."

This is not undermining hope. Hope can be defined as a confident, mental expectation of good, and it is extremely important. You will never have faith if you do not have hope (although you can have hope without having faith). I remember once being so despairing that I almost lost every vestige of hope I had. It is terrible to be in a place where you are without hope.

Hope is important, but hope alone is not enough. For years I lived in the future, countless times saying to Shirley, "One day I'm going to be different. One day Jesus will heal me. One day I'm going to be free." But it was always ahead somewhere, out of reach, like the proverbial carrot dangled before the donkey. What I thought was faith was only hope.

As you have been reading this book, hope has come to many of you. Your mind has received positive expectations of good and blessing. You are saying, "At last I can see there is an answer for me." If you are now to bring what you are hoping for into your experience, you must channel your hopes through the channel of faith.

Now may the God of hope fill you with all joy and peace in believing, that you may abound in hope by the power of the Holy Spirit. — Romans 15:13

Some say, "Lord, when I have joy and peace, I will believe."

But the Word says to believe and then joy and peace will come. Don't put the cart before the horse.

The Operation of Faith

To operate faith to receive the blessings of God, there are principles we need to know and follow. Of course, through obedience to God, blessings come upon us without our even asking; but the answers to certain physical, mental, and spiritual needs will only be found by pressing in to God and receiving them by faith.

Expressed simply, the principles of operating faith are (a) receive by praying, and (b) establish by saying.

In Mark 11, by cursing a barren fig tree, Jesus taught His disciples how to operate faith. Let us look carefully at this passage:

. . . when they had departed from Bethany, He became hungry. And seeing at a distance a fig tree in leaf, He went to see if perhaps He would find anything on it; and when He came to it, He found nothing but leaves, for it was not the season for figs. And He answered and said to it, "May no one ever eat fruit from you again!" And His disciples were listening.

. . . .

And whenever evening came, they would go out of the city. And as they were passing by in the morning, they saw the fig tree withered from the roots up. And being reminded, Peter said to Him, "Rabbi, behold, the fig tree which You cursed has withered." And Jesus answered saying to them, "Have faith in God. Truly I say to you, whoever says to this mountain, 'Be taken up and cast into the sea,' and does not doubt in his heart, but believes that what he says is going to happen, it shall be granted him. Therefore I say to you, all things for which you pray and ask, believe that you have received them, and they shall be granted you." — Mark 11:12-14; 19-24

(a) Receive by Praying

In the Mark 11 passage just quoted, Jesus said, . . . *"All things for which you pray and ask, believe that you have received them, and they shall be granted you."* The progression is (1) "pray and ask," (2) "believe," and (3) "shall be granted."

(1) "Pray and ask": Knowing that it is God's will for us to be free, and knowing that Jesus Christ has provided a complete redemption for us through Calvary, we are to ask the Father in Jesus' name for our deliverance once and for all.

(2) "Believe": Having asked for the provision, Jesus said, "Believe you have received." Faith is *now*. I believe I have received. Even though I cannot see the provision, even though I feel unchanged, I believe I have received. The evidence that the provision is mine is my faith — faith that has come through the Word.

(3) "Shall be granted": *Shall* speaks of the future. We have already received the provisions by faith; but they *shall* be granted at a later time. They are ours now in the unseen realm, but not yet ours in the seen realm.

Because you have the answer by faith, you no longer keep asking for it. To keep asking is evidence that you have not by faith received it. No more asking, but thanking and praising God that what you asked Him for is yours. Faith is your evidence. Faith relates to the unseen realm and "sees" the provision as yours — now!

The Holy Spirit will then release into your experience what you received when you prayed. But time is often involved: perhaps hours, days, months, and sometimes years. In the waiting, testing period you are to maintain your confession of possession by praise and thanksgiving. If you are merely parroting principles, you will be disappointed; but if you have this truth operating from your spirit, you will receive it in experience no matter how long may be the delay.

Understanding this faith principle was the turning point for me. Thousands upon thousands of times I had asked the Lord for healing and deliverance, but never had I believed that I had received the answer. Now I came to the Lord to make one final request. When I began to pray, my imagination became alive. In the heavenlies I saw an enormous "bank" with every provision (blessings gained through the Cross) for the human race, and I saw a small account with my name on it. As I asked, believing I was receiving, I envisaged the Lord taking from His vast bank a small amount of provision — the answer to my small needs — and placing it in my personal account. The answer was mine! Healing, deliverance — mine! Not yet in earthly experience, but in heavenly places. Why? Because I believed I had received it when I prayed. What was my evidence? Faith in my heart. It was faith that was to increase as I continued to meditate upon the Mark 11 passage, and daily thank the Lord (no more asking) for what I had received *by faith*.

My prayer went something like this: "Heavenly Father, I have asked so many times that You would change me, deliver me. But now I see that I haven't been releasing faith. I've been putting the responsibility on You to change me, while all the time You've been

97

waiting for me to use my faith to partake of what Jesus gained for me at Calvary. Lord, I come to ask You one final time. Please set me free from the bondages of the enemy. I ask You in Jesus' name for this provision. Lord, I receive my deliverance now. I receive complete salvation for every part of me. Your Word says: 'When you pray and ask, believe you have received,' and I believe, and I now receive. The provision is now in my account in the heavenlies. I never need ask again. I praise You. I thank You. By faith I am totally free. The bands of darkness are loosed. I am free! Jesus, my Deliverer! Thank You."

When I prayed this with understanding, something happened inside me. The victory that was always ahead of me came into my spirit. Deep inside I knew the victory was mine, even though I was still just as bound. Now I was going to battle Satan's demons, not *for* the victory, but *from* the victory. Never again did I ask God for my deliverance. I simply kept thanking Him that it was mine.

When this turning point came, I was feeling very low, and apart from an awareness of victory in my spirit, I remained feeling low. I continued thanking God for the victory for three weeks before I noticed any change. When it came, it was very, very small, and yet it was a change — just a minute awareness that I was a little freer. I was encouraged to keep moving on in faith. I had received by praying, and Jesus had said that if I did that, then the provision would be granted.

That you may not be sluggish, but imitators of those who through faith and patience inherit the promises.   *— Hebrews 6:12*

(b) Establish by Saying

Weeks and months went by. Slowly I became stronger in myself, yet not much freer. It was then that the Lord taught me that by intelligently engaging in spiritual warfare, I could work with Him to release His answer more quickly. Certainly, by faith, I had received Calvary's provisions; yet I was still very bound.

Five years previously, spirits had come to the surface in an evident way with cryings and tearings in my body, but excepting for a few occasions, they had since "lain low." They had hidden themselves, and at times had even tried to tell me, via thoughts in my mind, that they weren't there.

Now my confession expanded. Instead of just thanking the Lord for freedom, I confronted the hidden strongholds. I named the areas of bondage and declared them defeated. I commanded spirits of darkness to leave me, declaring they now had no legal ground in my life. For some months I continued in warfare in this way without outward manifestations, but gradually noticed more freedom coming.

Then came a further turning point in which the Lord gave me clearer insight into how to break demonic strongholds. As I maintained my confession of faith and declaration that the works of Satan had no part in me, I began to "see" what was happening inside me. I became aware of the names of the spirits that God was dealing with as I prayed. I "saw" their reactions, their resistings, their weakenings, and their breaking up. As spirits rose and left me, I "saw" them going. Before long I realized that the gift of "discernings of spirits" was beginning to operate in my life.

Through this the Lord has taught me from personal experience how to successfully overcome satanic bondages. One important thing I learned was the power of *speaking* to areas of bondage and in Jesus' name commanding release. I saw how the spirits reacted to the words I spoke.

There is tremendous power in the spoken word. God created the world simply by speaking words. He rules the entire universe by the power of His word. If He chose to, He could speak one word and the entire universe would be obliterated. Jesus spoke to the wind and the storm and it instantly obeyed Him. He healed and delivered by speaking words. We launch our spiritual weapons through speaking.

In the Scripture passage under consideration, the fig tree withered and died because Jesus *spoke* to it. Our faith is to be released in words and actions. Jesus *said, . . . "May no one ever eat fruit from you again!" And His disciples were listening.* Why? Because Jesus was *speaking*.

The next day when they again passed the fig tree, Peter expressed amazement that it had withered and died. Jesus replied with these powerful words: . . . *"Have faith in God. Truly I say to you, whoever says to this mountain, 'Be taken up and cast into the sea,' and does not doubt in his heart, but believes that what he says is going to happen [literally "believes that what he says happens"], it shall be granted him" (Mark 11:22-23).*

Probably, as He spoke, Jesus turned to a nearby mountain; not that He meant us to remove literal mountains, but He was highlighting the fact that anything — any kind of obstacle — could be removed by the word of faith. Even though the sickness or bondage may seem as immovable as a solid mountain, yet when the "mountain" is spoken to in Jesus' name, with the speaker not doubting, but believing that what he says is happening as he says it, it shall be removed — what the person says shall indeed happen!

What is said now is one of the most important things in this book: **As you confront demonic bondages, speaking in Jesus' name, and using the weapons of your warfare, you must believe that what you say, happens. It is happening as you say it. Faith is NOW!**

Remember the measure of faith. Our measures are different. Yours may be greater than mine, but we can each use what we have. Because Jesus had the Holy Spirit without measure (John 3:34), He also had the gift of faith without measure. He could move a mountain with one word. You and I may not be able to move mountains as quickly as Jesus did, but we can get the same results by removing them little by little using the measure of faith we have. As you speak the word of faith to the demonic stronghold, you could perhaps see yourself moving the mountain with a bulldozer, or if your measure of faith is not great enough for that, then see yourself moving it with a pick and shovel. The key is: believe that what you say happens. This is releasing your faith. This is how you please God. Strongholds are weakened and broken by this means. You don't have to feel full of power or tremendously spiritual. Feelings don't come into it. It is by faith we overcome.

If you intelligently confront the source of your problem (your mountain), using your weapons of warfare, and believing that the Holy Spirit is taking your commands and quickening them to be powerful, and believing that what you say is happening as you say it, and continuing day by day to confront and move the mountain, then little by little it will fall away. Slowly and surely your faith will flatten the great mountain. Brother and sister, you can remove mountains!

God said to His people:

Behold, I have made you a new, sharp threshing sledge with double edges;
You will thresh the mountains, and pulverize them,
And will make the hills like chaff.
You will winnow them, and the wind will carry them away,
And the storm will scatter them;
But you will rejoice in the Lord,
You will glory in the Holy One of Israel.   *— Isaiah 41:15-16*

Chapter 9

New-Creation Realities

When as a young Christian I set out on a Bible memorization program, one of the first verses I learned was 2 Corinthians 5:17:

Therefore if any man is in Christ, he is a new creature; the old things passed away; behold, new things have come.

Having given my life completely to Jesus Christ, I was aware of many wonderful changes within. Yet my deepest needs were not being met. As the months turned into years, I became extremely disappointed that I was not the "new creature" the Bible talked about. For some unknown reason it seemed that the truth of this verse did not work for me. Feeling I was not being honest, I gave up quoting it. The reality of it was "out of my reach."

Today, however, this truth is precious to me. Through deliverance I have now become a new creature in experience.

I am sure many of you will identify with this out-of-reachness of being a new creature, even though you rejoice in the measure Christ has changed you. To understand why our experience of what we are in Christ often does not line up with what the Word of God says, we need to understand how we are made and how God works in us to release the life of His Son.

Man a Tripartite Being

The Bible teaches that man is a tripartite being, that is, one who is made up of three parts: spirit, soul, and body.

Now may the God of peace Himself sanctify you entirely; and may your spirit and soul and body be preserved complete, without blame at the coming of our Lord Jesus Christ.

— I Thessalonians 5:23

It is easy to distinguish our body from the rest of our being, but perhaps a little more difficult to distinguish soul from spirit. Although our spirit and soul are closely aligned, there is a definite dividing of

101

the two. Hebrews 4:12 says: *For the word of God is living and active and sharper than any two-edged sword, and piercing as far as the division of soul and spirit, of both joints and marrow, and able to judge the thoughts and intentions of the heart.*

What then are the differences between our spirit, our soul, and our body? What are the faculties of each? And how do they function?

Our **spirit** enables us to have God-awareness through the faculties of communion, intuition, and conscience.

Our **soul** enables us to have self-awareness through the faculties of mind, emotion, and will.

Our **body** enables us to have world-awareness through the five senses of seeing, hearing, touching, tasting, and smelling.

Generalizing, we could say: *God* dwells in our spirit (after conversion). *Self* dwells in our soul. Our *senses* dwell in our body.

Our *spirit* contacts the spiritual world. Our *body* contacts the material world. Our *soul*, the real you and me, stands between the two worlds and can experience both of them.

To be a balanced Christian we need to cater for each part of our whole make-up. We should not major on one part to the detriment of another.

Man at Creation

When God created man, He made him a living soul: *Then the Lord God formed man of dust from the ground, and breathed into his nostrils the breath of life; and man became a living being [AV: soul] (Genesis 2:7).*

Man was made in the image of God. God is spirit and also formed in man a spirit, thus lifting him above the level of the animal creation to be able to experience fellowship with Himself, the Creator.

Then God said, "Let Us make man in Our image, according to Our likeness; and let them rule over the fish of the sea and over the birds of the sky and over the cattle and over all the earth, and over every creeping thing that creeps on the earth." And God created man in His own image, in the image of God He created him; male and female He created them. — *Genesis 1:26-27*

Adam and Eve enjoyed constant communion with God. Harmony filled their lives. They enjoyed complete absence of sin, sickness, and bondage. Each part of their whole being — spirit, soul, and body — was fulfilling its created function.

Death Through Sin

And the Lord God commanded the man, saying, "From any tree of the garden you may eat freely; but from the tree of the knowledge of good and evil you shall not eat, for in the day that you eat from it you shall surely die."
— Genesis 2:16-17

Tragically, Adam rejected God's Word and the moment he did so, he died. Not physically, but spiritually.

Through sin, Adam's spirit lost contact with God; he became "dead" to God. The line of communication was broken; the stream of life cut off; the light within turned to darkness. The corruption of death then began to work in Adam's soul and body. Although he did not die physically until he was 930 years old, the outworking of this death began the moment he died in spirit.

God had created Adam to exercise dominion over the earth and its creatures. In yielding to Satan's word, Adam not only fell from fellowship with God, but he lost his right to rule. Satan snatched Adam's position of authority and became ruler of the world (John 14:30). From that moment on, the human race came under Satan's domination and lordship.

Adam's sin had far reaching consequences. It affected every generation of mankind:

Therefore, just as through one man sin entered into the world, and death through sin, and so death spread to all men, because all sinned.
— Romans 5:12

Jesus — the Last Adam

The first man, Adam, failed to introduce God's purposes in the earth. Instead of life came death. God, therefore, purposed to send His Son, the second Adam, who through obedience to the Father's will would bring to birth, by the Spirit, a new race of people who would be as Himself, walking in obedience and loving righteousness. 1 Corinthians 15:45-48.

In the fulness of time, God sent His Son into the world, born of a virgin by an operation of the Holy Spirit (Galatians 4:4; Matthew 1:18-25). As the Son of Man, He lived as a man and was subject to all the pressures and temptations of life that we are subject to; the difference between ourselves and Jesus being that He never once sinned. Not being of the seed of Adam, the corruption of sin was not at work in Him as it is in every child born in Adam's line. God was His Father, the source of His life, and from and in that source, He lived.

Jesus Christ came to this world to die. He came to offer Himself as a substitutionary sacrifice for the sin of the world. Having no sin Himself, He could offer Himself to the Father on behalf of a corrupt humanity. As a sinless offering, He could take upon Himself the sin of the world and the judgment due because of it. In so doing He could release man from the penalty due him. Isaiah 53:3-6.

The Victory of Jesus

What in the natural seemed a terrible tragedy, turned out to be a great victory; for in dying and rising from the dead, Jesus not only dealt with the corruption of sin, but broke the legal right of Satan to dominate the human race. He triumphed over Satan and all his hosts.

When He had disarmed the rulers and authorities, He made a public display of them, having triumphed over them through Him.
— Colossians 2:15

Jesus Christ "disarmed the rulers and authorities" (literally "He put off from Himself the principalities and powers") and triumphed over them. The word *triumph* speaks of more than just gaining a victory. In ancient Rome many a returning, victorious general would ride in his chariot to the Capitoline Hill to be honored for his victory. In the procession and on public display would be the defeated and chained captives of his warfare plus the spoils of his conquest. When Jesus Christ defeated Satan and his hosts, He made a public display of them — a display viewed particularly in the unseen realm.

John simply states: . . . *The Son of God appeared for this purpose, that He might destroy the works of the devil (1 John 3:8).*

Although Satan has been defeated, he does not like to concede defeat. As believers, we are to enforce the victory of Calvary over him, and to take the ground he still holds through his deceptions and wickedness.

Identification in Death, Burial, and Resurrection

It is wonderful to know that Jesus died for our sins that we might be forgiven. But do you realize that we have been more than just forgiven of our sin? The Christian life is not to be a continual sinning and being forgiven, then sinning and being forgiven. When Jesus died **we died in Him** that the power of sin (and therefore Satan) might be broken.

Knowing this, that our old self was crucified with Him, that our

104

body of sin might be done away with, that we should no longer be slaves to sin; for he who has died is freed from sin.

— Romans 6:6-7

When Jesus died on the cross, our "old self," our sinful Adamic nature, was crucified with Him. When Jesus died, we died. This is an accomplished fact. Our old self *was* crucified with Him. It's past! It's completed and we are to believe it.

When Jesus was buried, **we were buried with Him**: *Therefore we have been buried with Him through baptism into death . . . (Romans 6:4).*

Someone who is dead and buried is unaffected by sin's enticements. You can wave a bottle of wine before the face of a drunkard who moments before collapsed and died, but there will be no response. As much as he would have desired a drink when he was alive, now he is dead, he is free from the power of alcohol and does not respond to it.

Brothers and sisters in Christ, we are to identify, by faith, in death and burial with Jesus Christ. We are to say to the temptation of sin and the allurements of the devil: "You have no power over me. I have died to sin. I have died to this temptation. Satan, you cannot touch me; for when Jesus died, I died in Him. When Jesus was buried, I was buried in Him. I am dead to sin; dead to your dominion; for in death I have died to every hurtful desire and I have been freed from this present evil world."

But let's go further. Jesus did not stay in the grave. He rose in newness of life and ascended to His Father's throne to rule and reign. **We have been raised in Him** to resurrection life.

For if we have become united with Him in the likeness of His death, certainly we shall be also in the likeness of His resurrection.

— Romans 6:5

We are to begin to reign over the works of darkness. Not later, but now. Not after death, but in life.

For if by the transgression of the one, death reigned through the one, much more those who receive the abundance of grace and of the gift of righteousness will reign in life through the One, Jesus Christ.

— Romans 5:17

We are to rise up against demonic bondages and say: "I have died to the dominion of the powers of darkness, and I now live and reign as a child of God. I use my authority in Christ to overcome you. I live in resurrection power. I walk in Holy Spirit anointing. I cut the bonds. I set myself free; for I am seated with Christ in the heavenlies.

105

I share His victory. I share His triumph. Thank You, Lord, for the power of Your Spirit flowing right now releasing resurrection life within me."

But God, being rich in mercy, because of His great love with which He loved us, even when we were dead in our transgressions, made us alive together with Christ (by grace you have been saved), and raised us up with Him, and seated us with Him in the heavenly places, in Christ Jesus. — Ephesians 2:4-6

As you persevere in breaking bondages in your life — and this is a progressive task — also declare who your new Head is: "I am a child of God and Jesus Christ is my Head. I am no longer in Adam, but in Christ. The power of Adam's inheritance has been broken over me; for I have been redeemed by the precious blood of Christ. Old things *have* passed away. All things *have* become new. Every bondage transferred through the family line from generation to generation is broken. I am free. I am in Christ. I receive the blessings of His inheritance. I am joined to Him. I am new now. I see myself totally free (or healed) because of Calvary. I believe the Word that being in Christ I am a new creation. Hallelujah!"

This daily confession releases the Holy Spirit to work deeply in you to bring these realities to pass. You are to speak with understanding, not merely verbalizing Bible truths, with your heart out of step. You are to speak in faith. As you maintain such confession, the Holy Spirit will enable you to enter more and more into the understanding of these truths as well as into the experience of them.

Alive in Spirit

With these truths before us of victory over sin and Satan through identification with Jesus Christ, let us now see how God works salvation in our lives.

As said previously, man is a tripartite being made up of spirit, soul, and body. God, being Spirit, works upon and through our human spirit to influence our soul life and our physical body.

First, our spirits have to become alive to God. In John 3 Jesus emphatically told Nicodemus that a man could not see or enter the kingdom of God unless he was born again (literally "born from above"). This new birth, this receiving of new life, has to do with man's spirit. When a person turns to Jesus Christ in true repentance and faith, acknowledging Him as Lord, an inward miracle takes place. The Holy Spirit enters man's human spirit and dwells there.

When Adam sinned, his spirit died to God, but now through the new birth, man's spirit becomes alive to God. He receives forgiveness of sin and the gift of eternal life. He becomes a child of God.

In my own experience, when I wholeheartedly turned to Christ as Lord and Savior, it was as if a light were turned on, on the inside. I felt clean inwardly and was aware that a great pressure lifted from me. The Bible became a living book. Creation became alive in a new way, even to noticing the singing of the birds. I was a nature lover, a bird watcher, and yet everything became alive and new to me. This may not be your experience, but it was how I was affected. Within my heart was a witness, a knowing that I had passed from death to life.

The Spirit Himself bears witness with our spirit that we are children of God.   — *Romans 8:16*

Do you not know that you are a temple of God, and that the Spirit of God dwells in you?   — *1 Corinthians 3:16*

Our spirit is located somewhere in the region of our "belly," that is, the area below our diaphram and above the pelvis. Proverbs 20:27 says: *The spirit of man is the lamp of the Lord, Searching all the innermost parts of his being.* Also in John 7:37-39 Jesus said, . . . *"If any man is thirsty, let him come to Me and drink. He who believes in Me, as the Scripture said, 'From his innermost being [literally "out of his belly"] shall flow rivers of living water.' " But this He spoke of the Spirit, whom those who believed in Him were to receive; for the Spirit was not yet given, because Jesus was not yet glorified.* Ephesians 3:16 speaks of being . . . *strengthened with power through His Spirit in the inner man.*

Having become alive in our spirit, the faculties of our spirit begin to operate.

The faculty of **communion** operates, for it's from our spirit we worship and enjoy fellowship with God. Jesus said, *"God is spirit, and those who worship Him must worship in spirit and truth" (John 4:24).* Only by our spirits do we touch God.

Also the faculty of **intuition** begins to work. We become aware of knowing things that do not come to us by natural learning through the processes of the mind. Either by scriptures being quickened to us, or words or impressions settling on our heart, we begin to hear the voice of God. When God called me to Canada, He spoke to me when I was waiting in line in a fish shop. I was communing with the Lord in my heart, knowing He was directing us to take a further step in Him, but not knowing where; when to my surprise the country of Canada was strongly impressed upon my spirit. This is knowing intuitively. It is receiving guidance or illumination by the Holy Spirit speaking to our hearts.

Then too our **conscience**, the faculty which enables us to discern right and wrong, begins to find new expression. By knowledge stored in our mind in the soul realm, we make many judgments which are not necessarily correct. Now, by an operation of the Holy Spirit applying the cleansing blood of Jesus within, our mind and conscience are released into truth and can begin to function properly. Our human spirit possesses the function of conscience, distinguishing right from wrong.

God works from the inside out. He first dwells in our spirit, and from there reaches out to renew our soul and our body. As we grow spiritually, our spirit finds more and more release.

It is possible to be born again of God's Spirit, and baptized or filled with the Holy Spirit, and yet be gripped by bondages or sick in body. If God is in us, why is this? If Christ is in our hearts, why is it that we can have a bitter sarcastic tongue, or be filled with jealousy, or be gripped by fears, or overcome by sexual lusts, or feel drawn to suicide? It is because these bondages are in the soul realm. The Holy Spirit can indwell our spirit, while evil spirits still have a place in our soul or body. To release ourselves from bondage, we have to submit ourselves to God and cooperate with the indwelling Spirit of God.

Renewed in Soul and Body

In our human soul are the faculties of mind, emotion, and will.

Our **mind** enables us to understand. By our reasoning faculties we rationalize, deduce, judge, etc. Our imagination enables us to produce mental images of what is not present or has not been experienced. Our memory is able to store and recall past sensations, thoughts, knowledge, etc. Our mind is a marvelous faculty and it is the main area of Satan's attack.

2 Corinthians 10:3-5: *For though we walk in the flesh, we do not war according to the flesh, for the weapons of our warfare are not of the flesh, but divinely powerful for the destruction of fortresses. We are destroying speculations and every lofty thing raised up against the knowledge of God, and we are taking every thought captive to the obedience of Christ.*

Many satanic strongholds are firmly entrenched in minds and need to be broken down with spiritual weapons. Not every thought in our mind stems from ourselves. True, multitudes of our thoughts do, and others come from the indwelling Holy Spirit or from other people putting thoughts there as in a conversation. But many thoughts can also come from indwelling demons that have made their abode in the mind. As they inject their thoughts into our minds, unless we recognize them, we accept them as our own thoughts and in so doing are being guided or influenced by the enemy. Satan can also attack from outside us, and put thoughts into our minds. However, I believe that many of the "mind" or "thought" problems that Christians have are caused by demons *in* the mind rather than outside the mind.

In one area of my life I confessed "my sins" to the Lord many times daily. Whenever certain thoughts were in my mind, I felt condemned and unworthy to be a Christian. How I confessed and claimed forgiveness! After some years I realized that I was not the source of these thoughts. Their origin was demonic. I also realized that just because I was tempted did not mean that I had sinned. I began to speak against the source of the thoughts, against a stronghold in my mind, and as I persisted month after month, I gradually came into liberty. I had been deceived for years into accepting "evil thoughts" as coming from my "evil heart!" How subtle is the enemy!

Our **emotions**, the organ of affection, the feeling part of us, can also be bound in varying degrees. Spirits of rejection make us "feel" rejected as well as speaking into our minds: nobody loves you. Spirits of self-pity play havoc in our emotional area — also spirits of anger, lust, addiction, pride, jealousy, etc., etc.

Also our **will** can be weakened or bound to varying degrees. We may know the right response, but be unable to make it. In the early days of my own deliverance, knowing the importance of reading the Word of God, I would sit down and try to reach out to pick up my Bible; but there were times of such powerful uprisings of demonic activity within me that I could not reach out. I would sit there, trying to, but couldn't. This happened on a number of days. It may sound foolish, but it was very real at the time. In my weakened physical and spiritual state, I was so overwhelmed in my will, that although I chose a course of action, I couldn't carry it out.

Our soul, being our self-realm, is a very important part of our being. It is also the main area of demon entrance and activity. Romans 6:13 says that we must choose constantly to yield ourselves to God for righteous purposes. The enemy knows when we are not being 100-percent for Christ and are giving him a legal right to work in our soul.

Some of you may be caught on a merry-go-round. With all your heart you are endeavoring to identify with Jesus and give no place to the devil; but through lack of freedom, you are constantly falling back into a particular sin. When you fall, you feel condemned and unworthy. You claim cleansing, you rise up to walk with God again, and then — crash! This is repeated, rising up and falling down again and again even though you hate falling.

Let me encourage you. Without in any way condoning sin, know that God sees your heart. He sees the great battle you put up, and then sees you fall. Remember He sees your heart as well as the outward action. Continue to stand against the sin with your whole strength, but if you fall, quickly claim cleansing and rise up. Do not let the enemy put further condemnation on you. Rather, keep resisting the enemy and keep breaking the inward bondage through spiritual warfare. Sooner or later you will rise in freedom and get off the merry-go-round.

Then there is the realm of our **body**. Much physical sickness and weakness stems from sources in the realms of spirit and soul. We could say that our spirit is sheathed within our soul, and our soul is sheathed within our body. We have witnessed many physical healings as people have been delivered from spirits binding the soul realm bringing them stress and tension.

There are other health problems that are caused by spirits of infirmity that directly attack the body. My own breathing difficulties disappeared when I was delivered from spirits of infirmity.

Although there is much physical sickness within and without the church, the physical problems, as great and real as they are, represent only a small portion of the total needs of man. Beneath the surface of the physical, in the realm of the soul, lie man's greatest needs. In displaying its tip, an iceberg shows only part of its real size. Its major bulk is far beneath the water. Man's physical needs can be likened to the tip of the iceberg.

When our bodies and souls are in bondage, it greatly affects the release and functioning of our spirits. Certainly, when we are believers, God is within; but He needs to touch our bodies and be released into our souls through our faith and cooperation with Him.

New-Creation Confessions

As members of a new creation, we must begin to speak the new-creation language. On our lips must be the truth of God's Word.

Jesus Christ is the great high priest who represents us before the throne of God. He is the high priest of our confession:

. . . consider Jesus, the Apostle and High Priest of our confession.
— Hebrews 3:1

Since then we have a great high priest who has passed through the heavens, Jesus the Son of God, let us hold fast our confession.
— Hebrews 4:14

As we confess (the Greek *homologeo* means "speak the same thing, assent, accord, agree with") what the Word of God says we are, Jesus Christ is released in His priestly ministry to work on our behalf to bring the truths of our confession into our experience.

Conversely, if we do not maintain a right confession, but speak of defeat, negativity, worthlessness, lack of power, etc., His "hands are tied" and He cannot work for us.

Revelation 12:11 says: *And they overcame him because of the blood of the Lamb and because of the word of their testimony, and they did not love their life even to death.*

Listed following are Bible verses that declare what we are in Jesus Christ. Know them, memorize them, and meditate on them. Confess them audibly even if you don't "feel" you are what they say you are. Satan may tell you that you are lying, but take no notice of him. Let God's Word be in your heart and on your lips. Through the working of the Holy Spirit, your continual faith confession will bring these truths into your experience. Add to the list other scriptures you find that teach you who you are in Christ.

1. I am a new creature in Christ.
   Therefore if any man is in Christ, he is a new creature; the old things passed away; behold, new things have come.
   — 2 Corinthians 5:17
2. I am a child of God, an heir of God, and a joint-heir with Christ.
   The Spirit Himself bears witness with our spirit that we are children of God, and if children, heirs also, heirs of God and fellow heirs with Christ. . . .   *— Romans 8:16-17*
3. I am delivered from Satan's dominion.
   For He delivered us from the domain of darkness, and transferred us to the kingdom of His beloved Son.   *— Colossians 1:13*
4. I am free from condemnation.
   There is therefore now no condemnation for those who are in Christ Jesus.   *— Romans 8:1*
5. I am seated with Christ in the heavenlies.
   And raised us up with Him, and seated us with Him in the heavenly places, in Christ Jesus.   *— Ephesians 2:6*

6. I am blessed with every spiritual blessing in the heavenlies.

    Blessed be the God and Father of our Lord Jesus Christ, who has blessed us with every spiritual blessing in the heavenly places in Christ. — Ephesians 1:3

7. I am more than a conqueror.

    But in all these things we overwhelmingly conquer through Him who loved us. — Romans 8:37

8. I am complete in Him.

    And in Him you have been made complete, and He is the head over all rule and authority. — Colossians 2:10

9. I am His workmanship.

    For we are His workmanship, created in Christ Jesus for good works, which God prepared beforehand, that we should walk in them.

    — Ephesians 2:10

10. I am healed of all physical diseases.

    But He was pierced through for our transgressions,
    He was crushed for our iniquities;
    The chastening for our wellbeing fell upon Him,
    And by His scourging we are healed. — Isaiah 53:5

11. I am appointed to go and bear fruit.

    You did not choose Me, but I chose you, and appointed you, that you should go and bear fruit, and that your fruit should remain, that whatever you ask of the Father in My name, He may give to you. — John 15:16

12. I am an ambassador for Jesus Christ.

    Therefore, we are ambassadors for Christ, as though God were entreating through us; we beg you on behalf of Christ, be reconciled to God. — 2 Corinthians 5:20

13. I am an able minister of the new covenant.

    Not that we are adequate in ourselves to consider anything as coming from ourselves, but our adequacy is from God, who also made us adequate as servants of a new covenant, not of the letter, but of the Spirit; for the letter kills, but the Spirit gives life.

    — 2 Corinthians 3:5-6

14. I am endued with power by the Holy Spirit.

    But you shall receive power when the Holy Spirit has come upon you; and you shall be My witnesses both in Jerusalem, and in all Judea and Samaria, and even to the remotest part of the earth.

    — Acts 1:8

Chapter 10

Self-Discipline and Deliverance

Self-discipline is a vital aspect of deliverance. If we are to gain our freedom, we have to wholeheartedly come against the enemy. This means aggressive spiritual warfare. Once hidden holds are exposed, it is costly to break from them.

Because different individuals have different abilities and potential, we cannot always compare one person's response to another's. Some are more bound than others. But however extensive the bondages are, the Lord sees our hearts. He knows the response we make, and so too does the enemy. The Lord does not require us to make a response beyond our capacity, but He does require wholeheartedness. To face deliverance with a casual, give-it-a-try attitude is inadequate.

In my own quest for release, before the truth of deliverance was revealed to me, I was highly disciplined, doing everything I knew to do my part to find God's help. Too many Christians want the blessings on a silver platter. They want the Lord to do it, or the counselor, or the pastor; but they won't do their part.

Some people see deliverance as an easy way out of their problems. They think that all they have to do is go to someone with a deliverance ministry, receive prayer, and be delivered of all bondages. They expect then to wake up and find they are a totally changed person with all their problems solved. Such people end up disappointed and often go from one person to another, hoping to find someone "spiritual enough" to help them. Deliverance does not work this way. God wants us to do our part.

A young man came for counsel and deliverance. His history was one of mental breakdown, drug addiction, and attempted suicide. Many times I had counseled him and urged him to seek employment in his area of qualification; I had rebuked him for stealing from a

113

Christian roommate and so on. As he shared his continuing needs, I asked him if he was seeking the Lord regularly. (He was still unemployed and had ample time to pray and read the Word.) Upon a negative response, I said I would not pray for him until he began to discipline his life and spend a regular period of time daily in waiting on God. Instruction followed on how he could do this. "When you are doing your part, return, and then we can pray."

Some weeks later he returned, and when I asked him if he had been seeking God, he replied that he had been listening to some Christian music. I refused to pray for him.

Finally he came again, having made some token response to the counsel given. I prayed and some release took place; but upon placing the responsibility on him to continue to do his part, my counsel went unheeded. He wanted it all to happen "now" and without any strain on him. He was a sluggard and will remain a captive for life unless he starts to do his part.

If we are to rise up in liberty and strength, we must be cultivating regular fellowship with God through prayer and meditation in His Word. We must walk in the light, being fully obedient to Him. If the problem area is resentment and bitterness, we must not flow with every wave of bitter emotion. We must choose to forgive those who have affected us. Every time resentment rises inside, we must choose to resist it; choose to have a positive response instead of a negative one. We can pray the Lord's blessing on our former "enemies." By continually choosing to love rather than hate, we are preparing the ground for deliverance; we are weakening the enemy's hold even though resisting him may be extremely difficult. From this stand of obedience and self-discipline, one can then name the offending area and begin to set oneself free from the demonic source.

There are some Christians who believe only in self-discipline (of course, with God's help), and not in deliverance. They give counsel such as: Try harder. Control your mind. Use your will power. Stop worrying. To a person in need of deliverance, this can bring great frustration and condemnation.

There are, however, some people who do gain a measure of release and victory in their lives solely through self-discipline. Even non-Christians sometimes overcome problems in this way, but they are usually strong-willed people. Because they are applying the Bible principle of resisting evil, a certain measure of victory can come. In my own life, this was not my experience. I disciplined myself rigidly, and yet I was not overcoming.

There are other people who through self-discipline and always choosing to do the right thing, acquire an outward veneer of righteousness. They come to a place where outwardly they are going through all the motions of doing the right thing, but inwardly they are fighting a terrible battle. Some Christians think this is how the Christian life is. They think they have overcome the flesh, when outwardly they can keep the flesh under control. I once heard it said of a certain Christian, "He has a violent temper, but he is a marvelous Christian and keeps it under control." God sees our heart, not just our outward veneer. He wants to cleanse us from within. Freedom is being able to worship God and live for Him without being faced with a constant inner battle.

Just before we left Australia to come to Canada, a friend sought counsel, saying she wished she had come to us years before instead of waiting until the last minute. She confessed she was continually depressed and unhappy and had been for years. This woman was jovial and outgoing, held a responsible job, and gave no outward appearance of her inward need. She was known to all as a happy person. When we prayed, some very strong holds began to surface and break.

Within Christian circles we too often deceive one another. We are told that Christians have peace and joy and don't have any problems. But behind the Sunday smiles are many aching hearts. Testimonies are given that are positive and sound wonderful. The Christian life seems to be nothing but joy and blessings; but so often the other side is not told. Let's be honest with ourselves. Unless we are, we will never come into the full freedom Jesus has for us.

People at times come to me and ask for discernment that they might know more clearly the areas of need they are trying to overcome. This can be helpful, but it is not necessary. You yourself know at least some of the areas in which you have problems. Right now, why don't you take pencil and paper and write down areas of inward need in which no matter how much you've tried, no matter how much you've disciplined yourself, confessed your sin, or prayed for God's help, you have not been able to get victory. Don't try to find things that aren't there. Perhaps someone may write:

Depression: Much better than I used to be, but still have some difficult days.

Fear: Don't enjoy being with others, although I want to be with them. Can't relax in their presence. Have always felt inferior.

Asthma: Had this since I was a child. It has eased since I became a Christian, but last month I had a bad attack.

Fingernail Biting: Wish I could stop. I've tried hard. Even wore gloves at home for a while to try to break the habit.

Etc., Etc.

Now let's be honest: Behind the depression are spirits of depression. That gripping fear is caused by spirits of fear. The asthma will be healed when spirits of infirmity are cast out. Your fingernail biting has its source in spirits of insecurity or other related spirits. Know your enemy. Know his tactics. Discipline yourself to rise up against him, clothed in the armor of God, wielding the weapons of your warfare. Don't accept these problems as just part of you. Begin to speak to the **source** of each of these need areas:

Depression: "In Jesus' name I bind and break all depression and *every related spirit* at the source of this bondage." I say "related" because one family of spirits supports or strengthens another. Depression may be linked to self-pity or regret, and so in coming against "depression and every related spirit" we are releasing the Holy Spirit to deal with all types of spirits at the source of the bondage.

Fear: "In Jesus' name I bind all fear working in my life. *Every kind of fear* hindering my relationships with others I weaken and break. All inferiority, embarrassment, insecurity, shyness, etc." (The Holy Spirit can bring to your understanding the key types of fear you should be naming.)

Asthma: "I bind infirmity at work in my chest and *every related spirit* strengthening and stirring behind these asthma attacks. I break the *source* of this condition in my life in Jesus' name."

Fingernail Biting: "I bind the *source* of this habit. *Every kind of spirit* at the roots of this, I break in Jesus' name. All insecurity, all anxiety . . ."

Often as we begin our direct commands, having acknowledged the spiritual source of problem areas, some spirits really begin to stir. Don't be alarmed if things stir and you appear to be getting worse rather than better. Realize what is happening, and be encouraged that by the weapons of your warfare you are finally reaching the source of the problem area, and by faith and perseverance you *are* breaking through into liberty.

It is not until we begin to rise out of spiritual bondage that we realize the extent of the enemy's holds. While spirits have a "house" to live in, they are usually content and do not exert their full strength. However, once we acknowledge the spiritual source of a problem area

116

and commence to deal with it, the spirits become unsettled and resist our attacks. Because of the inward pressures caused by the stirring of the enemy, it is easy to become discouraged and not continue to break through into full freedom. When we stop our attacks, the enemy usually settles down again and the pressure within eases. Some conclude that it is easier to stay in bondage than to have "all the pressures and problems" that arise when they persevere in warfare. Is this the way of a conqueror?

Dealing with the source of problems in a spiritual manner does not overrule practical, natural steps that can assist to alleviate pressures. For instance, if you are battling with depression and the problem is accentuated whenever you become overtired, then get some early nights. If when struggling with asthma, you find relief through medication, then use it and don't feel condemned. There are many practical steps one can and should take, but remember that the source of a spiritual bondage needs to be broken with spiritual weapons.

Chapter 11

Physical Healing and Deliverance

Although this book does not major on physical healing, the truths enclosed are just as relevant for the releasing of the physical body as they are for the releasing of the soul. In the Word of God, the two are closely related.

When Jesus and His followers ministered to personal needs, deliverance and healing were linked:

And when evening had come, after the sun had set, they began bringing to Him all who were ill and those who were demon-possessed. And the whole city had gathered at the door. And He healed many who were ill with various diseases, and cast out many demons. . . . — Mark 1:32-34

And He called the twelve together, and gave them power and authority over all the demons, and to heal diseases. — Luke 9:1

And God was performing extraordinary miracles by the hands of Paul, so that handkerchiefs or aprons were even carried from his body to the sick, and the diseases left them and the evil spirits went out. — Acts 19:11-12

There are instances where it is directly stated that evil spirits were the source of physical sicknesses:

Then there was brought to Him a demon-possessed man who was blind and dumb, and He healed him, so that the dumb man spoke and saw. — Matthew 12:22

And when Jesus saw that a crowd was rapidly gathering, He rebuked the unclean spirit, saying to it, "You deaf and dumb spirit, I command you, come out of him and do not enter him again." — Mark 9:25

And behold, there was a woman who for eighteen years had had a sickness caused by a spirit; and she was bent double, and could not straighten up at all. — Luke 13:11

The Bible several times refers to deliverance as being "healed" or "cured" of evil spirits. Obviously many of the people who were "healed" of evil spirits were actually physically sick.

And also the people from the cities in the vicinity of Jerusalem were coming together, bringing people who were sick or afflicted with unclean spirits; and they were all being healed.

— Acts 5:16

And also some women who had been healed of evil spirits and sicknesses. . . . — Luke 8:2

At that very time He cured many people of diseases and afflictions and evil spirits. . . . — Luke 7:21

And behold, a Canaanite woman came out from that region, and began to cry out, saying, "Have mercy on me, O Lord, Son of David; my daughter is cruelly demon-possessed." . . . Then Jesus answered and said to her, "O woman, your faith is great; be it done for you as you wish." And her daughter was healed at once.

— Matthew 15:22, 28

Demoniacs, or as we would call them today, the "mentally ill," were cured through deliverance:

And the news about Him went out into all Syria; and they brought to Him all who were ill, taken with various diseases and pains, demoniacs, epileptics, paralytics; and He healed them.

— Matthew 4:24

The demoniac who had a Legion of spirits (Mark 5) was "in his right mind" or "healed" after Jesus cast out the spirits.

When spirits of infirmity are the source behind a sickness, before there can be permanent healing, the spirits must be cast out of the afflicted area — either driven out by direct commands, or through gifts of healings, or the workings of miracles. The source of many physical conditions can be traced back to fear, resentment, guilt, etc., and only as these spirits are cast out, will healing be experienced.

There often needs to be both deliverance and healing — first deliverance, then healing. When Jesus healed the woman who for eighteen years had had a sickness caused by a spirit, He first cast out the spirit (*"Woman, you are freed from your sickness"*), and then He laid His hands on her and she was healed (Luke 13:11-13). In her condition, her spine would have become fused together, so that even after the spirit was cast out, a healing or re-creating would have been necessary. Thus Jesus first delivered, then healed her.

Also in the case when Jesus healed the boy brought to Him because the disciples could not cast out the spirit, we are told that Jesus first rebuked the unclean spirit and then He healed the boy (Luke 9:42).

From experience I have observed that many believers pray for healing when they should first have been driving out the spirits of infirmity. We would see more physical healings if we had more rebuking of the enemy first.

Of course, if people abuse their bodies by overwork, overeating, lack of regular sleep or exercise, or by continually eating harmful foods, the key to their healing is caring for their bodies properly — not blaming the devil. Let's be wise.

I know a pastor who was instrumental in his wife being healed from terminal cancer. They had asked the Lord for healing, and believed they had received the provision by faith (Mark 11:24). For two years, while in the natural her condition deteriorated and there were days of severe suffering, they both maintained a confession of health and praised the Lord that she was healed "by His stripes." Then, in a service one Sunday, her husband discerned that behind the cancer were spirits of infirmity that were hindering the healing being manifested. With a fellow pastor, he rebuked the spirits of cancer and cast them out. From that moment healing began to flow. To the bewilderment of the specialists, later tests showed no trace of her ever having had cancer.

Suffering from the restrictions of asthma, a man accompanied by his wife came to us for prayer. He had received prayer for healing some weeks previously, but had experienced no relief. Immediately we took authority over the spirits of infirmity in his chest and started casting them out. Within minutes he was breathing so much more freely that I am sure he would have been content to have had no further prayer; but I continued praying for thirty to forty minutes until I sensed we had removed the whole stronghold. They were both de-lighted and praised God he had been healed. We then spoke the word of healing to any area damaged by the spirits. Recently I met this man again (nearly two years had passed) and he had not had a trace of asthma since. He *was* healed and *is* healed.

Chapter 12

Manifestations or No Manifestations

When demons are cast out, they frequently manifest in most unpleasant ways: loud cries, screams, convulsions, etc. This happens today just as it did in the days of Jesus. Spirits cry out in fear because they have been uncovered and are no longer secure. They loathe having to leave "their house" to go into "dry places."

And demons also were coming out of many, crying out and saying, "You are the Son of God!" . . . — *Luke 4:41*

And throwing him into convulsions, the unclean spirit cried out with a loud voice, and came out of him. — *Mark 1:26*

And after crying out and throwing him into terrible convulsions, it came out; and the boy became . . . like a corpse.

— *Mark 9:26*

For in the case of many who had unclean spirits, they were coming out of them shouting with a loud voice. . . .

— *Acts 8:7*

There is no need to hide the fact that manifestations occur. We should not be perturbed if they cause an unscheduled interruption to a church service. Neither should we fear that the unsaved will be driven away by what may appear to be unseemly behavior. Rather than be afraid or disturbed, we should rejoice that the kingdom of God has come amongst us.

While I was conducting a deliverance meeting, without my knowing it, an unsaved couple came to the Lord. Rather than being offended by the manifestations, they themselves began to receive deliverance, one of them having to rush to the washroom to vomit as deliverance was received. They were thrilled at what the Lord was doing in the congregation and for them personally. They said they

123

would never again doubt the reality of the power of Jesus Christ or the reality of the unseen powers of darkness.

When Jesus set the captives free, He did so in public places — a street, a synagogue, a home, a hillside — just wherever the need surfaced. He was not concerned that what was happening was unusual, that religious protocol was being disturbed, or that people were being put off spiritual things because He was not being religiously respectable. He had come to do the Father's will and He was doing it. John 4:34. God's ways are not our ways, and God's methods are not always our methods.

Jesus said, . . . *"I do nothing on My own initiative, but I speak these things as the Father taught Me. And He who sent Me is with Me; He has not left Me alone, for I always do the things that are pleasing to Him" (John 8:28-29)*. He was so in touch with the Father, so conscious of the spiritual realm, so sensitive to what Satan and his hosts were doing that He boldly exposed Satan's work and dealt him a crushing blow.

Although we should not be disturbed by manifestations, neither should we go to the other extreme and take delight in them. I do not delight in seeing manifestations for manifestations' sake. Rather, I teach and encourage people to receive deliverance as quietly as possible.

Many demons leave without any manifestation. When praying for deliverance, we should not look for manifestations or expect that they will always occur. Who wants to see a display of demon power? It is far better if they leave quietly.

Deliverance — even great deliverance — can be experienced without any outward or inward felt reactions. Manifestations are not a necessary evidence that deliverance is taking place. One in every three or four people whom I pray for in counseling sessions, never feel anything happening. Yet the Lord can be doing great things. At the end of a session they may feel physically tired or they may feel no different at all. They would not know by their senses that any spirits had left them. This is why the gift of discernings of spirits is so important. By the Holy Spirit one can perceive what is happening or not happening inside a person. What is happening outwardly becomes unimportant.

Frequently, Christians come to me having been previously told by a pastor or counselor that they had no demons. Perhaps the counselor prayed for them in Jesus' name commanding spirits to manifest, and when nothing manifested, they were told they had no need of deliverance. Or they were told that Jesus' name is all-powerful and the spirits have to obey words spoken in His name. Because there was no response to the command, there were no demons to come out. This type of counsel can be devastating.

A young person came with great inner conflicts and began to receive deep deliverance. She told me that three years ago a minister had told her she did not need deliverance. She confided that because of the enormous struggles within her, she had made no spiritual progress since and had almost turned away from Christian things. "I've wasted three years of my life because I was told I didn't need deliverance," she said. In the following months, as she began to set herself free, her life blossomed into increasing freedom.

My heart goes out to people like this because I know what they have gone through. I was told myself by well-meaning counselors that I had no evil spirits.

In regard to manifestations, people receiving deliverance usually fall into one of three categories:
(a) Those who experience marked, traumatic manifestations.
(b) Those who have mild manifestations: sighing, coughing, belching, yawning, breathing heavily, feeling inward stirrings, heat, tension, etc.
(c) Those who feel nothing happening as far as their senses are concerned.

Some people fit into all the categories, receiving deliverance in different ways at different times. But I cannot stress too much: deliverance does not depend on our feelings, but on our faith. If we are speaking to areas of darkness believing that what we say is happening, there is an inside operation of the Holy Spirit weakening and breaking holds.

Let us look at each category:

(a) Those who experience marked, traumatic manifestations

This can be very upsetting when it first happens. Some people are embarrassed, and it can be very tiring. Faces and bodies are sometimes twisted into the most unusual positions.

The advantage of going through deliverance in this way is that you are encouraged because it is easy to see that God is doing something, and usually you feel much better after a breakthrough comes. However, if the manifestations continue, some pull out of the fight because of the cost involved. It is costly to break from the enemy's hold.

I sympathize with people in this category, because my deepest deliverances were very traumatic. As much as I tried to cut down the demonic manifestations, I found it impossible to get free in some areas without deep coughing and sometimes vomiting. I went through extended periods of this as deep strongholds surfaced. The cost was high, but the results are glorious.

(b) Those who have mild manifestations

Many people fit into this category. It is perhaps the easiest group to be in because you feel things happening without it being too traumatic, although mild manifestations may cause physical tiredness after long sessions of prayer.

When people in the first group learn to control the full manifestations, they may also come into this category.

(c) Those who feel nothing happening

If you are in this group, you are fortunate that you do not have the trauma of outward manifestations. However, because there is no evidence on the natural plane that anything is happening, you will require a higher faith level (especially initially) to believe that bands are weakening and breaking. As you continue in faith, you will notice changes taking place in your life. The last testimony in Chapter 20 will be an encouragement to you.

Spirits will hide if they can. Some people who feel nothing happening decide they have no need of deliverance and don't carry on. Some become cynical.

Often those who start in this group, end up identifying with those in the second or even the first group.

Again, let me say, these are general categories. In an hour of deliverance, one person may have deliverance in each of the three ways.

The Control of Manifestations

Some say manifestations are only psychological and insist they be controlled.

I cannot agree that manifestations are only psychological, and I do not agree that they should always be controlled. I do, however, say that sometimes they *can and should be* controlled. On the other hand there are times when they *can but should not be* controlled. And there are other times when it is *impossible* to control them excepting, of course, by ceasing to pray. In this whole regard we need to learn to cooperate with the Holy Spirit and be guided by His leading.

During a deliverance meeting I was led to come against spirits of guilt afflicting lives. (Spirits of self-condemnation and guilt are very common.) As I prayed people were set free, but I sensed a strong pressure from the Holy Spirit to continue to labor in this area. Finally, I said, "The Lord is wanting to do a deeper work in this area. Don't hold back, but work with the Lord and let Him have His way."

Unknown to me, a believer in leadership capacity was having a great inward battle. Spirits of guilt were stirring, and she knew that to get free, she would likely have to make a fool of herself in public. When I said not to hold back, she chose to cooperate with the Lord and get free, rather than maintain her pride. Immediately the spirits rose up with great manifestations and screamings. All attention in the meeting focused in her direction. I called everyone to stand against the powers of darkness, and as a congregation we took our authority. For ten minutes the commotion continued until there was a glorious release. She told me later that during the ten-minute battle, she was unconscious of what was happening. She could only remember a pastor at one time declaring the power of the blood of Jesus.

With this person, when the stirrings were first felt, she was able to control them. However, it was not the time to control them. By controlling them, she was holding the spirits in. She had to let go of that control and let the spirits manifest. Having done this, all control was lost. It was a particularly strong rising of the enemy in which she was almost unconscious of what was happening.

At the other end of the scale are those who, when they first experience demons reacting strongly within them, in fear, abandon themselves completely to the spirits, letting them have full sway. In so doing they experience all levels of screamings and body contortions. They make no effort to resist what the enemy is doing, and without realizing it, are cooperating with him.

A young woman had high pitched screaming manifestations every time she received prayer at altar calls during Sunday services. When she finally sought counsel, I told her that I believed she could get free without such intensity of manifestations. As we prayed, she discovered that by cooperating with the Holy Spirit, and not the evil spirits, she was able to greatly muffle the cries, but still receive release.

127

Some people feel they have to scream to get free. This is not so. Those who find spirits manifesting — particularly with loud cries — must learn to inwardly resist the enemy, and not let him have full sway as he goes out.

At the same time, do not hold spirits in by giving them no expression. If, when a person feels spirits rising, he determines not to let them tear him or use his voice to any degree, he may, by his rigid stand, hold the spirits in. You must learn through experience how much to hold back and how much to let the enemy have some expression. By learning this control, most people can experience releases with much less trauma. Less attention is thus attracted to the spirits.

Sometimes, especially in meetings, I go to people who are experiencing loud cries and speak firmly to them, telling them to take hold of themselves and not to let the enemy have his way. Some people who have rejection problems actually enjoy the attention they bring to themselves by these manifestations.

We must not go to the extreme of trying to stop every manifestation. If we do, we can cut across the work of the Holy Spirit and cause the demons to chuckle as they go down into hiding again.

The counselor needs wisdom to handle every situation as is appropriate.

How Demons Leave

Demons leave primarily through the mouth. The Hebrew word for "spirit" is *ruwach* and the Greek word is *pneuma*. Both of these words also mean "wind" or "breath." Spirits then can be likened to wind or breath. Many spirits come in through the mouth and go out through the mouth. They go with the breath.

Not all, however, go in this way. Spirits may leave through the hands, the feet, or other parts of the body.

While ministering during a meeting in Papua New Guinea, I laid my hands on a church elder. Unknown to me, this dear man had suffered severely in his left knee for some years. He could not stand for long without much pain. When my hands touched him, so he testified later, the spirits of infirmity in his knee went down his leg into his foot, but would not leave his body. In childlike faith he removed his left shoe, and the spirits went out through his foot. He was delighted. He had been healed!

A few days later at another location in Papua New Guinea, a man received deliverance through his head. The people have very fuzzy hair, and as the spirits left, there was such a sensation in his head that he thought he had lost his hair. Hurriedly he felt his head and was glad to find that he didn't need "hair restorer." When he related his experience to us later, we all had to laugh.

Generally though, spirits leave through the mouth, and when commanding them to leave, I usually tell them to go with the natural breath.

Releasing Your Faith

Let your natural breathing out be the point of contact for releasing your faith. You can say to the demons: "In Jesus' name I break your hold. Come up and out of your hiding places now. I drive you out. As I breathe, you are going. I expel you with the breath." Simply believe that "what you say is happening."

Sometimes when spirits are leaving, the person breathes deeply and heavily. This excessive expulsion of breath is not done by the person, but is caused by the spirits as they stir up and go out. When this happens regularly, some people feel that to hasten the deliverance, they should breathe heavily themselves the whole of the prayer time. This is not advisable because it can cause dizziness.

On the other hand, when spirits are stirring and coming out, it sometimes helps to have a period of "pushing out," when you purposely push from your stomach region and breath out heavily pushing your breath up and out. Times of expulsion like this, when you aggressively stir yourself to expel demons, can cause a greater release. For normal deliverance, however, let your normal breath be the releasing means.

Commanding Inwardly

When you are commanding, it is not necessary to speak to demons audibly. Inward commanding (speaking in your mind without speaking through your lips) is just as effective. In fact, often it is more effective.

Sometimes, as you declare audibly the power of the Blood, or are praising God, etc., the spirits will rise, but not go past your lips. Your praise or your declaration of the blood of Jesus Christ becomes a barrier in their way that they will not go past.

In a counseling situation, I encourage the counselee to major on inward commands, using spiritual weapons inwardly, while I and any other counselor be involved in outward commanding. From personal experience, and by perceiving through the discernings of spirits, I have learned that under normal circumstances more results are achieved this way than by having the counselee totally involved in outward renunciation.

Although I have the counselee major on the inward, I usually commence a deliverance session by asking him to audibly renounce the works of the enemy and confess Jesus Christ to be his Lord, etc. Also, for a few minutes, every so often during the prayer time, I encourage the person to join the counselors in outward, audible commands and declarations. We teach self-deliverance by a mixture of inward and outward rebuking.

Sometimes while people are commanding inwardly, I perceive that the spirits will only come out after the person has made a bold, audible renunciation of them. At times like this they won't move until the person speaks out.

From time to time a person may find he is tongue tied. The demons will not let him speak. You must encourage the person, however slowly, to speak the words. This especially applies when people forgive others. "I forgive my father." "I forgive myself." How often we've witnessed strong resistance to these confessions.

This mixture of inward and outward commanding, in conjunction with breathing out as a point of contact for releasing your faith, is one of the most important things said in this book to help you deliver yourself.

Chapter 13

Deliverance: How Long Does It Take?

What is said in this chapter is of vital importance if we are to understand how to pull down enemy strongholds.

Deliverance is progressive. It does not happen all at once. Time is involved in being set free. The more extensive the areas of bondage, the longer it takes to break them. Most believers have little or no idea how extensive is the infiltration of demonic bondage in their lives.

Six months after I discovered my own need of deliverance, I visited a pastor friend who enthusiastically shared what God was doing on the altar calls in his Sunday night services. Demons were manifesting and releases were taking place. "Why," he said, "it only takes a minute for a person to be set free from demonic bondage." I listened, but said nothing. If he could have seen the battles I was going through, I am sure he would have thought differently. Certainly people in his services were being set free, but they were receiving only a measure of release.

Deliverance begins when a person is born again of the Holy Spirit. At that time a measure of deliverance is experienced even though in most cases there is no deliberate casting out. Again, when a believer is baptized in the Holy Spirit, further releasing takes place. For some it is major; for others, very little. After being baptized in the Holy Spirit, many Christians begin to have inward problems and wonder why. Some even leave the Christian pathway because they can't handle things. What is happening is that hidden demons are becoming restless because the Holy Spirit is moving in a greater dimension in their lives. When the demons are pressured by the Holy Spirit, the believer himself feels the pressure within and cannot understand what is going on.

Deliverance may also be received when people are genuinely

131

slain in the Spirit; or during a time of laughter in the Spirit; or when people gather to praise God; or when spiritual gifts such as gifts of healings or workings of miracles are operating. As Christian workers, whatever our method or emphasis may be, let us work together against the powers of darkness.

Just before the Lord showed me the key of faith, I had a dream. It wasn't an ordinary dream, but a communication of God in the night that was clearly a "spiritual" dream. In it the Lord showed me that the deliverance I was yet to experience was going to be progressive. I went through the process of deliverance, seeing clearly the demonic powers, their forms, their actions, their ferocity, and their weakenings. At the instant I became completely free, I was caught up in the Spirit to another world and saw a small measure of its glory. Although asleep, this was the most wonderful experience I had ever had. When I awoke, I could not understand why Shirley was still sound asleep. I had been making so much noise, shouting and rejoicing with all my might, that I thought she would surely have heard.

In the dream God had spoken to me and truth had been imparted. In the midst of many a fierce battle that followed in later days, what the Lord had shown greatly strengthened me to continue pressing on. It had been placed indelibly on my heart and mind.

Moving Into Canaan

In many ways the taking of the land of Canaan by the Israelites, can be likened to a believer taking the land of his own life.

The land that God promised the Israelites was a wonderful land. Deuteronomy 8:7-9 describes it as a good land with a plentiful water supply, excellent for cultivation, rich in minerals, and a land where there would be no lack.

But there was one problem: The land was occupied by the Canaanites, the Hittites, the Amorites, the Perizzites, the Hivites, and the Jebusites (Exodus 3:8). These were wicked people. Their principal god was Baal and their principal goddess was Baal's wife, Ashtoreth who was the personification of the reproductive principle in nature. The worship of these gods involved the most terrible orgies. The temples were centers of vice. They were tended by priestesses who were prostitutes and by sodomites who were male prostitutes. New-born babies were sacrificed to Baal, and when a house was built, a child would be sacrificed and its body built into the wall to bring good luck to the family. These and other practices reveal the wickedness of these people.

To obtain the land, these wicked people had to be destroyed. The Lord told the Israelites that the land was to be cleansed and its wicked inhabitants completely wiped out. No sympathy or mercy was to be shown. Not one person was to be left alive. Deuteronomy 7:16-24.

But who was going to do it? God or the Israelites? The Lord continually said that **He** would drive out the enemy: *The Lord your God shall deliver them before you . . . (verse 23).* And yet He also told **them** to do it: *. . . You shall make their name perish from under heaven . . . (verse 24).* It was not God alone, or man alone, that would rid the land; but God and man working together. So too, with the land of our lives, we are to cast out the enemy, not in our own strength, but with the Lord working with us.

Spying Out the Land

When the Israelites were in the wilderness, Moses sent out twelve spies to spy out the land of Canaan (Numbers 13:17-33). Before they could attack, they needed to know what the land was like. If the people were weak, they could overcome them easier than if they were strong; likewise if they were few in number rather than many. If the cities had fortifications, they would require a different strategy from what they would if they were unfortified.

We too are to spy out the land of our life. Are there areas of bondage from which we can't get free, no matter how much we pray, read the Word, discipline ourselves, etc.? If so, then there is an enemy in the land. He may be weak or strong, few in number or many. Enemies are to be driven out. If we have an inferiority complex, let's be honest and call it what it is: an enemy in the land. Let's realize that the source of the continual outbursts of anger, which cannot be kept in no matter how hard we discipline our lives, is a hold of the enemy. Often as I pray for people, I discern spirits of anger. Some people get angry on the inside, but don't show it outwardly. No one would ever guess they had an anger problem. But the person knows, and the Holy Spirit knows too.

Faith Versus Unbelief

When the twelve spies returned, ten brought a negative report. They said that the land was certainly a good land — BUT! "The people are too strong for us. Their cities are large and fortified. There are giants in the land. By comparison we look like grasshoppers! We cannot go and fight against them." The other two spies, Joshua and Caleb, had a different report. They said, "We should go and attack the land now, for we are strong enough to conquer it."

Without doubt the enemy was strong; but what had the Lord commanded them to do? To go into the land and take possession of it. Ten said they couldn't — and didn't. God judged them for their unbelief: they were struck with a disease and died (Numbers 14:37). The Israelites heeded the negative report and were also judged. Over the next forty years, the Lord destroyed their generation in the desert. Forty days the spies were in the land, and forty years judgment was on the people. Everyone twenty years old and over perished, excepting Joshua and Caleb. They had returned with a positive report: "We are strong enough to conquer the land." They were believers. They entered the land and took possession of it.

Many Christians will never come into great release. They see the obstacles and panic. There is a great price to pay (especially for some) to move into complete freedom.

Entering by Faith

The forty years had passed and a new generation stood on the eastern side of the Jordan River with Joshua as their leader. God said to Joshua: . . . *"Arise, cross this Jordan, you and all this people . . . Every place on which the sole of your foot treads, I have given it to you . . . No man will be able to stand before you all the days of your life. Just as I have been with Moses, I will be with you; I will not fail you or forsake you. Be strong and courageous, for you shall give this people possession of the land which I swore to their fathers to give them"* (Joshua 1:2-3, 5-6).

"Arise, cross this Jordan!" But how could they? The river was at the height of flood. Nevertheless, the people chose to obey God. The priests carrying the ark led the way and stepped into the flooded river. As they did, their faith action released the hand of God. The river stopped flowing and the people went over on dry ground. They started their conquest — by faith!

Aggressive Warfare

After crossing the Jordan, a plan of aggressive warfare was put into action. First a central campaign to spearhead them into the land, then a campaign to the south, and later to the north.

The city of Jericho was the first obstacle to overcome. Around its circumference were two walls ten meters high and five meters apart. The outer wall was two meters thick, and the inner wall, four meters thick. It seemed impregnable — a mountain that could never be removed. But in obedience to the word of God and to the shout of faith, the walls fell down and the city was destroyed.

This victory heralded the beginning of the enemy's defeat and the children of Israel's triumph. The book of Joshua describes the many battles and victories of the Israelites, and the miracles of God in their midst. Working with the Lord, they took the land. City after city was destroyed; king after king put to death. Ruthlessly they destroyed the enemy.

Time Passes

Joshua 11:18 says that Joshua was at war for a long time. Joshua 12 names thirty-one kings who were destroyed west of the Jordan. Historians calculate that the time from when Jordan was crossed to when the land rested from war was five to six years.

In Exodus 23:29-30 the word of the Lord to Moses had been: *"I will not drive them out before you in a single year, that the land may not become desolate, and the beasts of the field become too numerous for you. I will drive them out before you little by little, until you become fruitful and take possession of the land."*

We must know and accept the fact that deliverance is progressive. The claiming of our lives will not be fulfilled in a moment of time, but little by little. I have not met one person who has instantly been set completely free from every bondage. Some have had such great deliverances, that they were sure they were totally free; but as time progressed, the Holy Spirit began to deal with other areas needing cleansing, sometimes to the amazement of the people as they began to realize the extent of what God needed to do in them.

If we were set free in an instant of time, we would never learn the ways of warfare, and thus would never be able to keep our freedom. We have to be taught by God how to take the land and how to keep it. What's the point of being set totally free, if we have no understanding of our subtle enemy and how to withstand him?

It cost the Israelites to subdue Canaan and it will cost you. Warfare is not pleasant in the natural or in the spiritual realm. How long will it take you to become completely free? I do not know. Every person is different and the time taken depends on the extent of the bondage and the willingness of the person to do his part to get free.

135

But you can be assured that as you take the land, however long it may take, you will know the wonderful results of increasing freedom.

I believe there is coming a time worldwide when the Holy Spirit is going to move in a far greater dimension than He is moving now. When this happens, there will be a great cleansing in the church and the time of receiving complete deliverance will be greatly accelerated. The Lord is going to raise up a people, powerfully anointed and wonderfully free.

Let us not sit back to await that day, but let us take the land now, using the measure of faith we already have. Let us stretch our spiritual muscles and learn to fly in the heavenly places, walking and talking as those who are more than conquerors.

Unconquered Land

Even though the land of Canaan rested from war, Joshua had not been fully obedient to the Lord. To a large degree, the land had been subdued, but there were still areas where the enemy remained (Joshua 13:1-6). These areas were thorns in the sides of the Israelites as the years went on. Some Christians come to a degree of freedom, but then settle for less than the total freedom. Let it not be so of us.

Many people find it hard to understand the fact that deliverance is progressive. All I can say is that there are certain spiritual truths that cannot be reasoned out with the natural mind; we can only understand them by revelation of the Holy Spirit. So it is with the understanding of spiritual warfare.

By and large the church of Jesus Christ is prayerless and powerless, and living much like the world, being captivated by the natural seen world, and lacking understanding of unseen realities. Because we are living at a level of spiritual experience far below where the Lord wants us to be living, we see things from a clouded perspective, and are puzzled. We must face the realities of the unseen realm as they really are. Great are the inward needs of multitudes of God's people, and time and patience are required to completely take the land.

David Anointed King

When King Saul was rejected by God from being king over Israel, God told Samuel He had chosen a new king from among the sons of Jesse the Bethlehemite. I Samuel 16. David was the one chosen, and while still a teenager was anointed by Samuel to be the new king. Although Saul had been rejected and David chosen in his place, Saul continued to rule for many years. It is calculated to have been at least thirteen years before David ruled Judah, and another seven years before he also ruled Israel. Until Saul died, David lived in danger of his life, with Saul many times trying to kill him.

Why did such a long time transpire? Why should David, the anointed one, have to suffer under the hands of Saul? Why should David have to become a fugitive and live in the hillsides? Why should he live in danger of his life? We can only say that God's ways are not our ways. Time is involved in all God's dealings with His people.

We would say that if David was anointed king, let him rule as king now. We would say, if we have turned to Christ as Lord, let every bondage be broken immediately. Let there be no passing of time, no costly warfare, no dying to the self-life. Let us enjoy the rights of rulership now — not later. But God's Word says that it is through faith and patience (time passing) that we inherit the promises of God (Hebrews 6:12).

The Rule of Jesus

Time is also involved for the enemies of Christ to be totally under His feet. Although at Calvary Jesus won a great and thorough victory over Satan and his forces, Satan still works furiously to resist God's purposes in the earth and in the church. In Hebrews 1:13 we read of the Father saying to the Son: . . . *"Sit at My right hand, until I make Thine enemies a footstool for Thy feet."*

The day is yet to come when everything in the heavens, and on the earth, and under the earth, will bow the knee and acknowledge that Jesus Christ is Lord (Philippians 2:9-11).

1 Corinthians 15:24-25 says: *Then comes the end, when He delivers up the kingdom to the God and Father, when He has abolished all rule and all authority and power. For He must reign until He has put all His enemies under His feet.*

From Calvary's victory to when all Christ's enemies are under His feet, *time* is involved. The outworking of His victory and rulership is progressive. As we as individuals rise up to rule and reign in every area of our lives, let us not be deterred by the passing of time. The pathway to a full deliverance is a progressive experience.

137

Chapter 14

Hindrances to Deliverance

To step out of satanic domination, we must give the enemy no place to have any foothold. While he can find legal ground on which to stand, he will not go. This is why people at times seek deliverance, but do not receive. It is, therefore, important that we consider carefully the things that give legal ground to the enemy.

1. Lack of Repentance

Repentance is fundamental to salvation. To be set free from any sin, we must repent. John the Baptist preached it (Matthew 3:2); Jesus preached it (Matthew 4:17); and He commissioned the church to preach it (Luke 24:46-47; Acts 2:38).

How repentance needs to be preached today! God will only permit us to go on to maturity if the foundation of repentance is laid. Hebrews 6:1-3.

Repentance signifies a change of mind. We are to turn from the pathway of sin. Our thoughts and actions are to harmonize with God's Word.

I once witnessed a tragedy because of lack of repentance. With a minister friend I visited the bedside of a woman with terminal cancer. Although much prayer had been offered by Christian friends, I had had an inner knowing for some time that she would die. When we entered the room, I saw a spirit of infirmity looking at me from the afflicted area. Its face was one of mockery and I knew why. Here we were, representing the Lord Jesus Christ, with ability to speak the word for her recovery, but through lack of repentance the enemy had legal ground to remain and afflict. Unless she repented, we were powerless to help her.

Shortly afterwards, we returned again. During our visit a fine Christian minister came and offered to pray for her. His prayer was beautiful, compassionate, rebuking the sickness in Jesus' name, but not anointed. He prayed out of sympathy, not in the Holy Spirit. Within my heart the Lord was saying, "It's too late. It's too late." I began to weep. How could I share with her what I felt in God? Who would believe the words that the Holy Spirit was speaking in my heart.

As we talked with her, we suggested that perhaps there was ground for the enemy. We mentioned an area of sin, but she could not receive it. When we left, she was singing praise to God and confessing that she was healed by His stripes. She died not long after.

Through situations like this, many Christians become confused. They question why a loving God could let such a thing happen; why He didn't respond to their faith; why so many prayers were not answered. If only we could see as God sees!

Let me make it clear, however, that when other Christians die in similar ways, it is not always because they need to repent. In the case of this woman, the Lord had long sought a response from her, but it was not given. Her continuation in sin and lack of repentance had opened the door and given legal ground for the destroyer.

On the brighter side, a young Christian man came out on an altar call to get right with the Lord. As I laid hands on him, I discerned a spirit of homosexuality. It was a major stronghold. (Remember, we can talk in the singular, but think in the plural.) While I was binding the spirits, he fumbled in his pocket and pulled out a piece of paper which he then tore and threw on the ground. With that, he fell backwards on the floor. As I placed my hand on his chest and continued rebuking, he slid from under my hand like melting butter on a hot frying pan. No part of his body had moved to initiate the motion; the demons transported him away from the impartation coming through my hand. Afterwards he told me that on the piece of paper was the phone number of a man he was to call for immoral purposes.

This man, by destroying the paper, was repenting and turning from his sin. It was as he did so that things began to happen. If you want to be free, you must turn from all known sin. You fool yourself if you think you can play games with any form of sin.

2. Unforgiveness

Another common ground for enemy occupation is the sin of unwillingness to forgive.

Deep wounds result in countless lives because of what others have said or done. Sometimes the offense has been of the most terrible dimension, and the person suffering feels he is justified in harboring bitterness.

Others do not harbor bitterness against someone else, but against themselves. They cannot forgive themselves for certain actions or for certain sins they have committed. Unforgiveness hinders deliverance.

"Forgive us our debts, as we also have forgiven our debtors," Jesus taught His disciples to pray. Then, to emphasize the importance of the truth, He added, *"For if you forgive men for their transgressions, your heavenly Father will also forgive you. But if you do not forgive men, then your Father will not forgive your transgressions"* *(Matthew 6:12, 14-15).*

Could it be any clearer? If you do not forgive others, your heavenly Father will not forgive you. Your unforgiveness gives legal ground to Satan. We are to forgive, not because we feel like it, but because we choose to obey the Lord Jesus Christ.

Matthew 18 relates the story of an unmerciful slave. It is the story that Jesus told in answer to Peter's question, . . . *"Lord, how often shall my brother sin against me and I forgive him?"* . . . *(verse 21).*

A king decided to settle his accounts with his slaves, one of whom owed him an amount equivalent to ten million dollars. Of course the slave could not pay, and so to meet the debt, the king ordered him to be sold with his wife and children and all his possessions. The slave entreated the king to be patient, promising he would eventually pay everything he owed. But unexpectedly, the king graciously released him of the complete debt.

Having been released, this same man found a fellow slave who owed him a small amount, the equivalent of one day's wage, and demanded menacingly that he repay him. Likewise came a plea for patience and a promise of repayment. But the cry was not heeded, and the fellow slave was thrown into prison till he should pay back everything. His action was reported to the king, who sent for him and said: . . . *"You wicked slave, I forgave you all that debt because you entreated me. Should you not also have had mercy on your fellow slave, even as I had mercy on you? (verses 32-33).* Filled with anger, the king put him in the hands of the "torturers" until he should pay back the whole amount. Concluding the story, Jesus said, *"So shall My heavenly Father also do to you, if each of you does not forgive his brother from your heart"* *(verse 35).*

In this parable Jesus clearly taught that if a Christian does not from his heart forgive his brother, his heavenly Father will put him into the hands of the torturers. In other words, God releases him into the hands of evil spirits. Unforgiveness gives legal ground for demons to bind and bring great distress.

While praying in a meeting for a woman who was having traumatic manifestations with no progress being made, I discerned she was harboring unforgiveness in her heart. She confessed this to be true and named members of her family. "Go home and get before the Lord," I said. "Repent of your sin and ask God's forgiveness, because you will not be freed until you are willing to forgive from your heart."

If you are deliberately harboring unforgiveness, God will see to it that you won't get free (no matter who prays for you) until you forgive.

By an act of choice, in obedience to the Word of God, you are to say: "Lord Jesus, I choose to forgive — and I do forgive. By faith I receive cleansing now. And in Your name I renounce every spirit of unforgiveness."

If you need to forgive yourself, you should say: "Lord, I forgive myself. Never again will I blame myself or reject myself for what I have done. You have forgiven me, and I forgive myself. I claim freedom from the effects of this. In Your name, I renounce every evil spirit that has kept me in bondage in this area. Thank You that You are beginning to set me free right now. Thank You, Lord."

It is important to understand that our ability to forgive does not depend on our feeling able to forgive. If in your heart you sincerely desire to forgive, then choose to forgive; speak words of forgiveness. If afterwards you find you still have feelings of unforgiveness, do not let the enemy bring condemnation. Instead resist the enemy. Say: "Enemy, I have forgiven (so and so)." Then come against the spirits of unforgiveness that are making you feel as if you haven't forgiven.

3. Unbelief

We have already considered the key of faith in Chapter 8, but because of its importance I refer you again to this chapter.

Faith is the key to receiving from God. In contrast, unbelief hinders you from receiving from God. We are told that when Jesus was in Nazareth, He did not perform many miracles because of the unbelief of the people (Matthew 13:58).

Unbelief hindered the disciples from being able to cast a demon from an epileptic boy. The father had to bring him to Jesus to cast it out. Afterwards when the disciples asked Jesus why they could not cast it out, He replied, . . . *"Because of the littleness of your faith"* . . . *(Matthew 17:20).*

Sadly, some choose not to believe because of the cost. It may be a deliberate choice or it may be done unconsciously. There is a cost involved in identifying with certain doctrines and experiences. They may be contrary to the accepted beliefs of our denomination. We may risk losing our position or our friends.

There are others who want to believe, but no matter how hard they try, they find they can't. This is a frustrating situation to be in. What is the cause and what can be done about it?

As a young evangelist, I took ten days of my vacation to pray and fast because I wanted to find the Lord as my Healer. I knew that He healed today — and how desperately I wanted to be healed. But I wasn't sure if healing was in the atonement, or if God intended that everyone could be healed. I had with me an excellent book on divine healing. Throughout the ten days, I would get small glimpses of truth, seeing clearly the truth I was seeking, and then it would vanish. A few hours later, I would see it again, but again it would disappear. As desperately as I wanted healing and wanted to believe, no faith could be released in my heart.

Years later I realized that spirits of unbelief had been blinding the eyes of my understanding. It was during sessions of deliverance that I became free to believe that healing was purchased through the atonement. The breakthrough came when I was delivered from spirits of infirmity. How they manifested and cried through me as the truths of the blessing of healing in the atonement were declared! It was the demonic resistance that convinced me that healing was mine through Calvary's provision. Once the spirits of infirmity had gone and I was healed, I could see clearly from the Word, truths I had never seen before. There had obviously been a deliverance from unbelief at the same time.

If you want to believe, but can't, you should begin to renounce spirits of unbelief. As freedom comes, your faith can then find expression in other areas in which you need freedom.

An evangelist friend shared with me that while he was preaching in a church, one of the leaders responded to a call for salvation. The man had been active in the church for twenty-three years, but not born again. When the way of salvation was declared, he cried, "I want to believe — but I can't!'' My friend realized that a spirit of unbelief was at work, and naming it, rebuked it in Jesus' name. Immediately the man fell to his knees crying out to Jesus to save him. My friend stood witnessing a thrilling conversion experience that would never have come about if he had not taken his authority over spirits of unbelief.

4. Fear of the Supernatural

Many Christians have a fear of the supernatural. Our walk is to be a supernatural one, but the enemy, through spirits of fear, holds Christians back from entering into it and receiving supernatural blessings.

This fear can manifest itself as either a fear of God or a fear of Satan — neither of which stem from God. There is a fear of the Lord which is a good thing and which Proverbs 1:7 describes as "the beginning of knowledge," but the fear we are here referring to, has a demonic source.

While praying for a Christian worker, the Holy Spirit showed me that he had a fear of God that was hindering his relationship with God. This unnatural, demonic fear had come through his strict church upbringing which had given him an unbalanced concept of the nature of God. He saw his heavenly Father as someone with a big rod ready to immediately punish any offender. He confided that he had trouble trusting God for the future because of a fear of what God might do to him. Together we renounced this demonic fear, choosing to see the Lord as He truly is and to love and trust Him implicitly.

Other Christians are "frightened" of the Holy Spirit, particularly of the gifts or manifestations of the Holy Spirit. The cause often stems from negative teaching they have received.

Unnatural fears of God are to be renounced. The Word of God is to be read so that through revelation knowledge, we might see how wonderful our God is and how intimate our relationship with Him as His children can be.

Other Christians are afraid of Satan; afraid of talking about him or his works; terrified of what the devil might do to them. In truth, it is our enemy who is afraid of us, but through deception he tries to reverse the picture. Let us renounce the fear of Satan; renounce the fear of the supernatural. Let us yield to God, the Holy Spirit, and be filled with His presence and power.

Jesus said, *"Behold, I have given you authority to tread upon* serpents and scorpions, and over all the power of the enemy, and nothing shall injure you" (Luke 10:19).

Never again confess fear, but declare your authority and start "treading on" the enemy.

5. Pride

... "God is opposed to the proud, but gives grace to the humble." Submit therefore to God. Resist the devil and he will flee from you.   — James 4:6-7

Pride keeps multitudes from entering the kingdom, and within the kingdom keeps multitudes from receiving deliverance. How humbling it can be to have to confess you have inner needs, or to have to share areas of bondage that are embarrassing or that you think will sound foolish.

We prayed for a woman who had such a fear of water that she was afraid to be baptized. With reluctance she would enter her swimming pool on a hot day, but never place her head under the water. If we weren't sensitive, we could laugh and say, "It's ridiculous! Fancy being afraid of water." After her fear was acknowledged, and it was broken in Jesus' name, she was gladly baptized. What a victory! But it would never have happened if she had not humbled herself and sought help.

Men, may I speak a word to you. Why is it that we won't humble ourselves and open up as readily as women do? More women seek salvation and deliverance than men. The reason is not that men are not in need, for their needs are just as great. I believe the reason is that we men are often not as honest as women, and not so willing to humble ourselves.

Don't let the enemy keep you away from blessing any longer. Humble yourself today. Humble yourselves, therefore, under the mighty hand of God, that He may exalt you at the proper time (1 Peter 5:6).

6. Lack of Wisdom

Unwise words and actions can turn people away from truth. A brother offended is harder to be won than a strong city, and contentions are like the bars of a castle. Proverbs 18:19

Any new truth that comes to an individual can be received with such excitement that he wants everyone to know about it. But not everyone wants to know or is ready to know. Untold damage can be done by zealous, wisdom-lacking Christians who try to force truth upon others. This can apply particularly to the truth of deliverance.

When any exciting truth is discovered, one's mind tends to dwell much on it for weeks or even months until it comes into balance with other truths. There is nothing wrong with an initial overemphasis provided it does not continue forever.

People become tired of hearing someone always talking on one subject. Be balanced. Be wise. Don't talk about demons all the time. Don't boast that you were delivered from so many demons last week and so many the week before. Unwise words or actions can turn away others whom the Lord desires to bring into new liberty.

If in the past you have had foolish, unwise things said to you about certain truths, do not allow the effect of those words to keep you from entering into blessing. Forgive those who have said unwise things to you and choose to receive the truth.

7. Lack of Perseverance

Some expect that years of problems can be solved in an hour of counseling. This is not so. Time is involved. Warfare is work. Extensive time periods can pass before all bonds are broken. Many become discouraged and weary along the way.

In the midst of the battles, we must learn to appreciate what the Lord is doing. It is easy to see what the devil is doing. But what is God doing and allowing in the seeming delays? Without becoming passive, we must surrender to His full plan and purpose for our lives. The Lord is more interested in what He is making us into than in our comfort. When we appreciate the sovereignty of God, we will lose the panic.

My own road was one fraught with many pressures, and often there were days when I wondered if I could continue on. Each day I spent considerable time breaking inward strongholds. This went on, not for days or weeks, but a number of years. Some of you may have to come along a similar path. However, do not become discouraged. If you keep pressing on in perseverance and faith, you will come through just as I have come through. Joseph's time in Egypt as described in Psalm 105:16-22 was a source of strength that helped me to press on.

It was the Lord who sent Joseph to Egypt and directed his pathways through years of sufferings. This innocent, God-fearing, young man went through deep valleys when he could have questioned *why* he had to suffer as he did and for so long. Verse 18 literally says: "His soul came into irons." He could have blamed the devil or he could have blamed God for his mistreatment. But in it all, he kept his eyes on the Lord, his heart attitude right, and was able to rise above the daily pressures. By his right attitude and faith, the Lord was able to fashion him as clay upon the potter's wheel. God had a purpose for Joseph that was far beyond his imagination; but before he could be raised up, he had to be abased. Verse 19 says: *Until the time that his word came to pass, The word of the Lord tested him*. Each one of us is also on trial. How will we respond? Will we panic or trust? Obey or disobey? See from man's vantage point or God's?

When the Lord had fulfilled His purposes in Joseph, he was released into a responsible position of rulership, that caused him to be a savior in God's hands to his family, and a key person in God's ongoing purposes for His chosen people.

I am sure as he looked back, even though he would not have wanted to tread the same pathway again, he was glad for what God had *made him* and what God was *doing through* him.

The Lord is preparing us to reign, not only in time, but also in eternity. He is fashioning us through trials and sufferings into those who will share His throne throughout eternal ages. Only those who are "overcomers" share that glory. As we persevere in overcoming the adversary in our own lives, and as our spiritual muscles are daily developed, we are preparing ourselves for His eternal purposes for us as His people.

Of Christ it was said: *Although He was a Son, He learned obedience from the things which He suffered. And having been made perfect, He became to all those who obey Him the source of eternal salvation (Hebrews 5:8-9)*.

147

Chapter 15

How To Set Yourself Free

Building on the foundations of the previous chapters, we can now move into the practicalities of self-deliverance.

Applying these principles is not a matter of methodically following point after point. You must grasp the principles outlined, and then act as the Holy Spirit leads you. Once you are adept in self-deliverance, you can be setting yourself free no matter where you are — kneeling in prayer, walking, working, driving.

When you know what you are doing, and the inward enemy also knows that you know what you are doing, deliverance at times can be automatic without you consciously being involved. Your general confession of liberty through Christ and your regular praise to the Lord are weapons being used by the Holy Spirit to weaken and break bonds.

1. Acknowledge Jesus Christ as the Deliverer.

Never forget that Jesus Christ is the Savior and Deliverer (Acts 5:31). He alone paid the price for your redemption, and He alone is strong enough to make that redemption real in you. Whether you are set free as you seek God alone or through the help of others, it is the Lord Jesus who brings the freedom. We set ourselves free, not in the sense that we do it entirely on our own, but in the sense that we work together with the Lord and it is our cooperation with Him that releases His delivering ministry to us.

As time goes on and you become skillful in wielding spiritual weapons, it is possible, without even realizing it, to start trusting in methods and principles instead of in the life source of those principles; to start having faith in your faith instead of in Christ, the Author of your faith; or to start having faith in your confession instead of in Christ, the High Priest of your confession.

As important as the following guidelines are, all your words and actions will be void of power unless you constantly acknowledge Jesus Himself as the Deliverer and depend totally upon the ministry of the Holy Spirit.

2. Yield Yourself Totally, by Faith, to the Lordship of Jesus Christ.

This is not a "religious act" that you do once and then forget. It must be the constant attitude of your heart. Jesus is your Lord. Your life is His. You are His property.

It may be helpful to commence with a firm audible confession: "Lord Jesus, I acknowledge You to be my Lord. You have called me to Yourself, and I gladly respond to Your call and purpose for my life. Consciously and willingly I yield every area of my spirit, soul, and body to You. I choose to walk in Your ways. I choose to be filled with Your Spirit. You are Lord."

If you have not been born again of the Spirit of God, then you need to come to Jesus, the Savior, and receive forgiveness of sins and the gift of eternal life. You must be willing to turn from every attitude and action of sin, and be willing from this moment on, to follow the Lord Jesus Christ with your whole heart.

If you are not sure how to come to God, you can use the following prayer, making it your own, and speaking from your heart: "Dear God, I come to You needing to be forgiven, and desiring to be right with You. I have counted the cost of following Your Son, and I am willing to follow Him with my whole heart. I confess that I have sinned against You, and I ask You to forgive me now. I believe that Jesus Christ died for me, bearing away my sin, and that He rose from the dead, having overcome the power of sin and Satan for me. I yield myself now to the lordship of Jesus. I confess Jesus Christ to be my Savior and Lord. By faith, I receive forgiveness and the gift of eternal life. Thank You, Lord Jesus, for saving me and for coming into my life."

One of the first acts of obedience to Jesus, upon giving your life to Him, will be to be baptized in water, publicly acknowledging your severance from the dominion of sin and Satan (Mark 16:16).

You will also need to ask the Lord Jesus, the Baptizer in the Holy Spirit, to fill you with His presence, that you might commence the Christian walk by the enabling of His power. Acts 2:36-41.

3. Be Aware of Satan's Defeat. He Has No Legal Right to Afflict You.

Colossians 2:9-15. Commence your warfare from an inward sense of victory through the Lord Jesus. You are not fighting for the victory, but from a position of victory that Jesus has already won for you. The hidden spirits you will be attacking are the defeated ones, because the price for your redemption has been paid in full. They know their defeat: you must know it. All your attacking of the enemy will be upon the grounds of Calvary's provision. Evil spirits have no legal ground to touch you (provided you are not deliberately yielding to some area of sin).

4. Claim by Faith Your Complete Freedom. Believe You Have Received.

Determine that the day of asking and asking God for help is over. Choose to rise up out of panic and defeat, and receive your freedom by faith. Jesus said: . . . *"All things for which you pray and ask, believe that you have received them, and they shall be granted you" (Mark 11:24).* [See Chapter 8.]

Once you have received your answer by faith, you will not need to ask again. From then on, you will speak words of declaration and commands, for we receive by praying and establish by saying.

5. Acknowledge the Source of Your Problem.

Acknowledge that behind the areas of need, with which you have struggled and from which you have not been able to break free, are evil spirits.

Being invisible, they easily hide. Concealment is one of their major strategies for taking advantage over us. The first few days or weeks of your breaking free (especially if you do not experience manifestations) will be crucial, because the evil spirits will likely try to convince you that they are not there. Thoughts such as, "I don't have any demons," may well come to your mind. They will put forward their thoughts as if you were thinking them yourself.

6. Begin to Attack the Enemy.

Using the authority you have in Christ, and equipped with spiritual weapons [Chapter 7], begin attacking an area or areas of

151

need. You could commence speaking like this: "In the name of the Lord Jesus Christ, I come against you hidden spirits and I bind your activity in my life. You can no longer hide below the surface because I now recognize what you have been doing. I bind you and renounce your works." Then speak directly to a specific area of need. If fear is your problem, say: "Spirits of fear, I speak directly to you. I drive you out of my life now. The blood of Jesus Christ has redeemed me. You have no legal right to touch me. You are leaving me now with every natural breath. Come up and out now. I loose myself now. Spirits of fear are leaving me now. By the power of the Holy Spirit I am prevailing now. Thank You, Lord Jesus, that You are taking my commands and making them as shafts of light against the darkness. I stand free. The blood of Jesus sanctifies me. I praise You, Lord. Spirits of fear are going now. Out with every breath. . . ."

It is helpful to begin this type of warfare with audible commands. There is no need, however, to shout. You can speak quietly. The anointing is not noise. After a few minutes of placing audible blows of command on the enemy, change to inward commanding. Major on inward commands, but from time to time speak outwardly. Remember, that many spirits go out through the mouth and nose with the breath. Sometimes they are hindered from leaving if you are speaking all the time. [Chapter 12]

If you have an area of pressure, but you don't know the name of the spirit or spirits that are manifesting, then say: "I come against the *source* of this pressure. Every kind of spirit pressing me now, I am speaking to you. Go in Jesus' name." You don't have to know the names of spirits to overcome them. When you don't know the name, speak to the source behind the pressure you are feeling. If you are unable to move in the gift of discernings of spirits, then it is important to know this. Speak to *every kind of spirit at the source* of the pressure.

7. Be Aggressive Towards the Enemy.

Remember that we have been told to *ekballo* evil spirits. This is a word of aggressiveness meaning "cast out, drive out, expel, thrust out, pull out, send away." As Jesus "cast out" the money-changers from the temple with a whip in His hands, let us rise up within and "cast out" the spirits defiling our bodies, the temples of the Holy Spirit.

152

8. Believe That What You Say Is Happening.

The key to your release is faith. We receive by praying and establish by saying. Jesus said we were to speak to the mountain (the area of obstacle) and believe that what we say is happening. [Chapter 8]

We may not have a large enough measure of faith to remove the whole stronghold in one command, but we all can believe a measure of weakening and breaking is taking place.

Mingle your commands with positive faith declarations. Be authoritative. "Enemy — out! I stand in victory! I stand complete in Jesus Christ! Every evil spirit on your way out! With every breath I expel you!"

If manifestations occur, don't panic, but rejoice. The enemy is stirring because he has been discovered. He is on his way out. Stand strong deep inside and continue commanding.

Recently I helped remove a thick brick wall using a sledgehammer. It took a team of men several days to complete the demolition. The wall didn't fall down immediately. At times we had to place blow after blow on an area before the bricks finally fell away.

The same thing can happen in removing spiritual hindrances. You may for a few minutes see your words simply weakening an area: "I stand against this stronghold of fear. Every kind of fear, I weaken you now. As I bind you, you are weakening. I bind you so tightly that you have no expression in my life. Your activities in my mind are bound. Your activities in my emotions are bound. I overcome you by the blood of Christ and the word of my testimony."

Having brought a weakening to the area, then begin to drive the spirits out: "With every natural breath, I now expel you. Come up and out in Jesus' name. You are leaving me now. Thank You, Lord, for the releasing I am receiving. . . ."

9. Use Your Imagination.

Your sanctified imagination can be of great assistance to you as you release yourself. See with your mind a picture of what is happening. There are different kinds of pictures that you could see.

Just simply a picture of a word can be good. If you are coming against spirits of fear, in your imagination, you could see written inside you the word, "FEAR." Let that word represent the stronghold of spirits. Direct your commands to that word and as you do, see yourself as speaking to the spirits behind the word.

You may envisage some type of stronghold: perhaps a fortress, a wall, iron gates, or chains. The Scriptures refer to bands, fetters, nets, snares, yokes, and strongholds. Take these and apply them to the spiritual plane: "I break every chain. I loose myself from every chain of fear in Jesus' name. . . ."

Perhaps you will see yourself as a soldier clothed in armor with a sword in your hand. When speaking words to the enemy, see yourself thrusting the sword into the enemy's ranks. Delivering yourself or others is warfare — spiritual warfare. This is, therefore, a good avenue in which to let your imagination be alive.

Jesus spoke of evil spirits considering human bodies to be "their house"; and He spoke of the house being "swept clean" (Matthew 12:44). You could picture your mind, for instance, being swept clean like a room in a house. "I set my mind free. By the power of the precious Blood, I sweep my mind clean of all fear. All uncleanness going. I sweep you out as rubbish. . . ."

10. Be Sensitive to the Holy Spirit.

As you are conscious that you are working together with the Lord, and as you experience the Holy Spirit, the finger of God, taking your words and anointing them; be open to be guided by the Holy Spirit. Don't strain for revelation, but be open for it. You may find that impressions are coming to your mind that you hadn't considered: pictures, or words, or a sense of knowing what to do next.

The Holy Spirit can also quicken the faculty of memory. While speaking against spirits of fear, you may suddenly remember something that happened many years ago that you had long forgotten. You may remember the day when you were humiliated before your class at school. It comes to your realization that this was when your embarrassment problems began. Or you may remember the time you were left alone in the house when your parents went out, and how it caused a fear of being attacked to come over you.

As these things come to mind, be more specific with your commands: "I continue to speak against all fear. Every spirit that found a place that day at school when I was humiliated before others, all embarrassment, all inferiority, leave me now. By the power of God's Spirit, I break your effects now. Every root of fear that gripped me because I was left alone, I address you, you are in my "sights," and I aim right into your midst. All fear of attack, all fear of being alone, I break you down; I root you out in Jesus' name. As I breathe out normally, you are going with my breath. Thank You, Jesus, for release."

11. Be Persistent in Breaking Bondages.

Bondages can be weak or strong. A weak hold can often be broken quickly, whereas a strong hold may take a long time. Remember that spirits work in families. There may be many spirits in the one stronghold.

Imagine breaking into a physical stronghold. Just breaking through the main doors does not take the fortress. There may be many different buildings or rooms on varying levels within those great walls. The strength of some spiritual strongholds are only realized when a person faithfully and persistently works on breaking them down. Much time may be involved till every last area is taken for the Lord.

Spend time regularly in spiritual warfare until you come into freedom. If you have great inward pressures, as was my experience, make it a priority daily to wait before the Lord in prayer, and in His Word, and in time given to warfare.

Don't allow the enemy to make you feel selfish because you are spending so much time "on yourself." The devil is very cunning. He will tell you anything to hinder you coming into freedom. The enemy used to tell me I was selfish, and I had to overcome it. I finally had to realize that I could not effectively help others until I was first in a place of freedom myself.

12. Understand That Pressure Begets Pressure.

While evil spirits have a dwelling place, they seem to remain reasonably content. But when pressure is put on them to leave, they are likely to display their strength.

It is like having a cat sleeping contentedly on your lap. While you let it remain, everything is calm. But decide to move it, and suddenly there comes a resistance. Out go the claws gripping into your clothes and flesh. The more you try to lift it, the deeper in the claws go.

This is how it often is when casting out demons. As you pressure them to leave, they begin to stir. Some of their manifestations can be extremely strong and may physically tear the person as they resist being forced to leave.

155

Although most manifestations cease immediately prayer ceases, some people find that even during the day, when they are not involved directly in warfare, certain manifestations continue: dizziness, headaches, tension, feelings of sickness, etc. People who experience this kind of thing may have many days of inconvenience and difficulties.

Once the enemy had been exposed and brought to the surface in my own life, my road to freedom was paved with pressures. Constantly I experienced physical pain that was very wearying. Some days there was severe tension within me. Other days I felt dizzy. When deep areas of release were about to happen I felt sick. Then, as I went into warfare, and as the deliverance took place, I often vomited deeply.

Some people who experience this kind of thing, find it difficult to press on. The battle can be even more difficult if you are living in a situation where those around you do not understand what is happening. All I can say is: press on, don't give up, and don't despair. Let the Lord daily strengthen you and then, like silver is refined in fire, you will come forth free from impurities.

Now a word to people who have no awareness of manifestations: You also could find you have days when you are not quite yourself. You may find you are easily upset or impatient or just somehow uptight. This too can be because of inner stirrings taking place in reaction to warfare.

Some people will not be aware of any manifestations or stirrings, either during or in between times of warfare. Do not let this discourage you. It is by faith that we are set free. We are not to look for physical manifestations or reactions. Don't let the enemy deceive you into thinking that nothing is happening.

13. Acknowledge What God Is Doing.

Already in Chapter 14 we have made brief reference to Joseph and his sufferings, all of which were ordained of God. A deep work of God was done in this young man that was fitting him not only for earthly service, but also for eternal service.

As we have the right responses to God, He will use all things to work together for our good. Don't misunderstand what I am saying, but He will even use demons to fulfill some of His purposes in our lives. God is sovereign, not the devil. As we rise up out of demonic bondages, we are learning to flex our spiritual muscles, learning to release faith, learning to exercise spiritual authority, and learning to rule and reign. All these things would not be happening if there were no pressures.

This does not mean that we are to be passive in regard to what Satan is doing, but we are to see Jesus as Lord, and realize that nothing is happening to us that He is not aware of and allowing.

In Paul's life, there was a time when the Lord used a messenger of Satan to buffet him to keep him humble because of the revelations he had received. The word *buffet* means "to strike with the clenched fist." He was under demonic pressure that was ordained of God. Three times he sought the Lord that it might depart from him. But in the midst of the pressure, the Lord said: . . . *"My grace is sufficient for you, for power is perfected in weakness"* . . . *(2 Corinthians 12:9)*.

There were times in my experiences when I felt I could no longer take the pressure of the enemy. At these crisis times, I wept in weariness before the Lord, but each time I found myself uttering a cry that surprised me and made me realize the work the Lord had done in me. My cry went something like this: "Lord, I choose Your will continually. You know of the pressures I cannot seem to continue to bear. You know I want to be out of them, but I confess You are Lord. My times are in Your hands. I choose Your purposes to be fully fulfilled, even if it means more suffering like this." After such responses, a settled sense that God was sovereign would be upon me, and a knowing that despite the enemy pressures, He was working His will through it all.

14. Maintain a Christ-Consciousness.

. . . Let us run with endurance the race that is set before us, fixing our eyes on Jesus, the author and perfecter of faith. . . .
— Hebrews 12:1-2

Even though you are battling spirits of wickedness, constantly acknowledge the presence and power of the Lord Jesus. Only as you remain Christ-centered will you be able to successfully fight through.

Keep His Word ever before you, especially portions of victory and comfort that are relevant to your situation. Regardless of how you feel, you must maintain your confession of completeness through the Lord Jesus. Let defeat and negative confessions be replaced by positive daily declarations of what you are in Christ.

Chapter 16

Praying for Others to Be Set Free

The following are suggestions that may be of help when praying for others. Do not be limited, however, to copying how someone else operates. Each counselor should develop his or her own way of ministering.

1. Sit the counselee in a chair, such as a dining-room-table chair, that has no arm rests. This makes it easy for laying on of hands.

2. In the first counseling session, it is important that the person is given opportunity to open up and share areas of need. This will take much time for some, little time for others. Be a good listener. Also, be careful not to make known to others outside the counseling room the personal things shared with you.

3. Acknowledge the presence of Jesus who according to His Word is with those who gather in His name. Matthew 18:20.

4. Encourage the counselee to audibly confess Jesus Christ as his Lord and renounce the works of darkness. If he cannot pray on his own initiative, let him repeat a prayer after you. Choose that the Lord's will for the counseling time will be fulfilled.

5. Lay hands on the person and believe that there is an impartation of life being released as you minister.

6. Begin to pray, as outlined previously, in the areas of need acknowledged. Be open to impressions from the Holy Spirit, and learn to flow as He guides.

7. As you audibly rebuke areas, have the counselee rebuking and cooperating inwardly.

8. Keep paper towels and tissues close by in case they are needed.

9. Keep in mind that many people experience no manifestations. This is not an indication that they are not being set free.

10. Be willing to spend time in praying. Part of the success of ministering to others is to take time. One or two hours can go

159

very quickly. Look to the Lord to teach you to know when to finish the time of counsel.

11. Be calm as you minister. There is no need to "shout" at the enemy even when he manifests. There may be times under the quickening of the Holy Spirit when you speak loudly; but for normal praying you can minister with a normal level of voice volume.

12. Keep the pressure of spiritual attack upon the area or areas with which you are dealing. You are in warfare against intelligent spirit beings. Be direct and authoritative.

13. Before ending a session, ask the counselee if he is experiencing any pressure within. If so, speak to the source of the pressure area, and break it before you stop praying, so the person leaves with a sense of encouragement, not discouragement.

14. Conclude by giving thanks and praise to God for what He has done. Be careful as a counselor to keep the person's eyes on Jesus, the Deliverer, and to ensure that Jesus is given the thanks.

15. Let the counselee know he is welcome to be in touch if he has any questions or needs further help. Some will need to have another time set aside for further prayer.

16. During your time of counsel be teaching the counselee the principles of self-deliverance so that he can learn to touch God for himself and not be always dependent upon you.

Desire Spiritual Gifts

Although a knowledge of counseling procedures is helpful, there is a higher dimension of ministering in which all counselors should desire to flow. It is the dimension whereby spiritual insight is received through the operation of spiritual gifts such as the word of wisdom, the word of knowledge, and discernings of spirits. Flowing in this dimension enables the counselor to be guided to the source and solution of the problem.

1 Corinthians 14:1 says: . . . *Desire earnestly spiritual gifts.* . . .

The word *desire* in the Greek means "to have a zeal for, to be zealous towards." The dictionary says that *zealous* means "filled with or inspired by intense enthusiasm or zeal."

Let us desire and be open to receive every enabling that God wants to bestow upon us. The more equipped we are, the more we will accomplish for His glory.

A Time to Rest and a Time to War

To break spiritual strongholds, we need not only spiritual strength, but also physical strength. When a counselee tires physically during spiritual battles, he is less able to exert himself in aggressive warfare.

There can come a time during a prolonged session when it is better to stop praying and recommence on another day when the person is refreshed.

But there are other times when even though the person is extremely tired, it is best to keep battling. Sometimes deep areas of bondage are only brought to the surface after prolonged periods of warfare. As they surface they may manifest with great strength and resistance. In the natural, the counselor, on seeing that the person is exhausted, may want to stop and let him rest. But at times such as this, *do not* rest. It is imperative when something major is surfacing, that has taken a prolonged battle to bring to the surface, that all those involved rise up with all their ability to resist and drive out the demons. By keeping the pressure on, a major breakthrough usually results.

If because of tiredness, the spirits are not dealt with, they will settle down again, and it may take much time and effort to bring them to the surface again at some later time.

During a fierce battle, keep encouraging the counselee not to give in, but to use all his determination till the break comes. However, do not force the counselee beyond what he is able. If he becomes too exhausted, you will have to stop and pray again on another day. In times of intense spiritual warfare we need to remind ourselves that the greater the battle, the greater the victory. The resulting freedom is more than enough compensation for the energies exerted.

Chapter 17

Maintaining Your Deliverance

How important it is to keep what God has given us! With confidence our freedom can be maintained if we constantly give heed to the following exhortations:

1. Do Not Fear the Enemy Returning.

In Matthew 12 Jesus tells us where evil spirits go when they are cast out, and how they desire to return to "their house."

Now when the unclean spirit goes out of a man, it passes through waterless places, seeking rest, and does not find it. Then it says, "I will return to my house from which I came"; and when it comes, it finds it unoccupied, swept, and put in order. Then it goes, and takes along with it seven other spirits more wicked than itself, and they go in and live there; and the last state of that man becomes worse than the first. . . . — *Verses 43-45*

Spirits can only return and bring others with them if the house is left unoccupied and vacant. As you are set free, consciously yield the freed areas to the infilling of the Holy Spirit. Let them be occupied with God's presence, so there is no room for spirits to return.

When there is a continuance or re-occurrence of a problem after deliverance, many Christians become condemned, feeling they have given opportunity for spirits to return. Rarely is this correct. What is happening is that further spirits in the same bondage area are stirring. Spirits work in families or groups. The breaking of their holds is progressive. Even though a major release has been experienced, there may yet be many other spirits to come out. Sometimes they lie low for months before they consciously bother you again.

You must see yourself progressing, not going back; becoming freer and freer, not more bound. If you are walking in the light and yielding to the Holy Spirit's infilling, evil spirits are not coming back. Rather, through your faith and through the ministry of the Holy Spirit, other spirits within are being stirred up to be driven out. When they feel the pressure, because they are in you, you also feel the pressure. Realize what is happening and don't fear the enemy returning.

2. Yield Daily to the Lordship of Jesus Christ.

Every day deliberately acknowledge Jesus as your Lord. Let your heart be set upon Him and desire to do His will. Romans 10:9-10; 12:1.

The continuous attitude of my heart is: "Lord, I choose Your will." To do the will of God is of utmost importance to me. I see myself as His property. I declare continually that I have been sanctified and set apart, by His blood, for His purposes. My commitment to Him is 100-percent. He is my life, and therefore the works of darkness know they are not welcome.

3. Be Filled with the Word of God.

Let the word of Christ richly dwell within you, with all wisdom teaching and admonishing one another with psalms and hymns and spiritual songs, singing with thankfulness in your hearts to God.

— Colossians 3:16

Regularly read God's Word. Every day let a portion of Scripture be in your mind for meditation. Counteract the enemy's fiery darts with the truth of God.

In particular, meditate upon the glorious truths of your identification with Jesus Christ as outlined in the Epistles. Let these truths be released through your lips.

Joshua 1:8 says: *This book of the law shall not depart from your mouth, but you shall meditate on it day and night, so that you may be careful to do according to all that is written in it; for then you will make your way prosperous, and then you will have success.*

The word *meditate* in Hebrew means "to murmur, to speak in an undertone." Whether it be quietly, or in a speaking voice, let us have upon our lips the Word of God.

Let us also sing the Word through psalms, hymns, and spiritual songs.

Paul said of Timothy, . . . *"From childhood you have known the sacred writings which are able to give you the wisdom that leads to salvation through faith which is in Christ Jesus"* (2 Timothy 3:15).

4. Be Filled with the Holy Spirit.

And do not get drunk with wine, for that is debauchery; but ever be filled and stimulated with the (Holy) Spirit.

— Ephesians 5:18 AMP

The Spirit-filled walk commences when a believer comes to Jesus, the Baptizer in the Holy Spirit (Luke 3:16), and asks Him to fill him with the Spirit. By faith (Galatians 3:5) he begins to receive and drink of the waters of life. From then on, he is to be continually "being filled" with the Holy Spirit.

If you have not been baptized in the Holy Spirit, you could pray a prayer such as this: "Lord Jesus, I come to You now, acknowledging You as my Lord and Savior. I desire to be filled with Your Spirit. I desire to know You more. Consciously and gladly I yield my entire self to You for the impartation of new life. Right now I ask You to fill me, and by faith I begin to receive. Thank You, Lord Jesus. You are imparting to me now. You are filling me now. I praise You. I worship You."

Already we have discovered that in the Hebrew and Greek the word *spirit* also means "breath" or "wind." Jesus breathed on His disciples and said, . . . *"Receive the Holy Spirit" (John 20:22).* Just as evil spirits can be expelled through the breath, so the Holy Spirit can be received through the breath. God breathed into Adam the breath of life (Genesis 2:7). Jesus breathed on His disciples. With your eyes on Jesus Christ as your Baptizer, you can utter the prayer given or a similar cry from your heart; and then as you breathe in normally, let that breathing in be the action of releasing your faith to receive. "I receive the Holy Spirit. I receive now. I breathe in the breath of God. I yield to God, the Holy Spirit. I allow Jesus Christ to empower me for His service. I receive."

For some people, the entering of the Spirit-filled life is a dynamic experience. To others, it is a quiet receiving by faith. Whichever way we enter this new walk, we are to daily yield to the Holy Spirit, walking by faith, not by feelings.

Being filled with the Holy Spirit is not to be equated with wonderful feelings of emotion — although these may certainly be experienced. Even in difficult times, when our feelings are low rather than high, we are still filled with the Spirit. Being filled is not dependent on feelings. Jesus was not feeling "high" when He faced Gethsemane and Calvary, but He was still filled with the Holy Spirit.

165

It was the Holy Spirit who gave Him the strength to go through the sufferings.

Let us receive the Holy Spirit by faith, and then let us daily walk by faith, being constantly "being filled" with the Holy Spirit.

5. Be Clothed in the Armor of God.

Ephesians 6:10-17. We have already spoken on the armor of God which is part of our spiritual equipment. Place it on by a confession of faith and keep it on. Live in your armor. [See Chapter 7.]

6. Be Continually Praising.

Through Him then, let us continually offer up a sacrifice of praise to God, that is, the fruit of lips that give thanks to His name.
— Hebrews 13:15

From our waking moments until the day closes, let our hearts and lips offer up regular offerings of thanksgiving and praise. Initially we need to cultivate this, but after a while it becomes a part of our life.

Let us choose to praise the Lord, regardless of pressures or battles. He is worthy to be praised. A praising Christian is a victorious Christian. No praise, no victory.

7. Deal with Sin.

As soon as we know that we have transgressed, let us quickly repent and confess our sin to the Lord.

If we confess our sins, He is faithful and righteous to forgive us our sins and to cleanse us from all unrighteousness. *— 1 John 1:9*

By continuing in any activity of sin, we give legal ground for evil spirits to enter. We cannot afford to be careless with sin or to grieve the Holy Spirit.

8. Be Alert to the Enemy's Tactics.

Having been made aware how spirits gain entrance [Chapter 6], let us be on our guard. If we sense they could be seeking a place in us, declare our freedom in Christ and resist them firmly.

Recently when walking through a shopping arcade, I was strongly aware of the presence of evil spirits; the atmosphere was so heavy. Within my heart I thanked the Lord for protection and quickly resisted the presence of the enemy.

Be of sober spirit, be on the alert. Your adversary, the devil, prowls about like a roaring lion, seeking someone to devour. But resist him, firm in your faith, knowing that the same experiences of suffering are being accomplished by your brethren who are in the world. — 1 Peter 5:8-9

9. Cultivate Right Relationships.

A new commandment I give to you, that you love one another, even as I have loved you, that you also love one another. By this all men will know that you are My disciples, if you have love for one another. — John 13:34-35

We love because we are commanded to, not because we feel like it. Work at personal relationships. Keep yourself from bitterness, jealousy, criticism, unforgiveness, etc.

If you feel wrong attitudes beginning to lay hold of you, deliberately renounce the enemy and choose to maintain right attitudes. Declare the enemy has no place in you.

Deal with the pressures quickly rather than let the enemy build up a hold over weeks and months.

10. Be in Fellowship.

Every Christian should belong to a "sheepfold." There is an occasional exception, for example, a Christian who lives in an isolated, out-of-the-way place. However, most Christians have no excuse for not finding a spiritual home.

Don't spend a lifetime searching for a perfect church. You won't find one. Join yourself to a good, Bible-believing, Holy Spirit-honoring congregation where you will receive spiritual nourishment and spiritual oversight.

There are too many "gypsy" Christians who will not settle and let their roots grow down. Wanderers are in danger of being deceived. Sheep need sheepfolds.

Members of the Body of Christ are to function within the Body. You cannot function within the Body if you are not joined to the Body.

And let us consider how to stimulate one another to love and good deeds, not forsaking our own assembling together, as is the habit of some, but encouraging one another; and all the more, as you see the day drawing near. — Hebrews 10:24-25

11. Walk in Humility.

. . . *"God is opposed to the proud, but gives grace to the*

*humble." Submit therefore to God. Resist the devil and he will flee
from you.*
— James 4:6-7

Because the Lord is constantly fashioning and adjusting us, we
need to have an attitude of humility that causes us to be teachable. We
should welcome adjustment, especially from those who are spiritually mature and over us in the Lord.

Many times I have witnessed believers who through pride and
stubbornness would not submit to wise counsel, and who have thus
brought much hardship upon themselves and opened themselves to
demonic bondage.

*Obey your leaders, and submit to them; for they keep watch over
your souls, as those who will give an account. Let them do this with
joy and not with grief, for this would be unprofitable for you.*
— Hebrews 13:17

12. Be Christ-Centered.

Let Jesus Christ be central in your mind. See Satan as small and
Jesus as large. Let your conversation be Christ-uplifting, not devil-
uplifting. Major on the realm of light, not the realm of darkness.

*If then you have been raised up with Christ, keep seeking the
things above, where Christ is, seated at the right hand of God. Set
your mind on the things above, not on the things that are on earth. For
you have died and your life is hidden with Christ in God.*
— Colossians 3:1-3

Do not fear becoming demon-conscious. Having come myself
through many spiritual battles, and being now involved praying
regularly for others for deliverance, I am very demon-conscious.
However, being demon-conscious has made me much more Christ-
conscious than ever I was before. It has been through a Christ-
consciousness that I have learned to overcome and maintain victory
over the enemy.

Jesus is our wisdom, our discernment, our power, our victory,
and even our life itself. We are to be caught up with Him.

Chapter 18

Deliverance for Children

Children, obey your parents in the Lord, for this is right. Honor your father and mother (which is the first commandment with a promise), that it may be well with you, and that you may live long on the earth. And, fathers, do not provoke your children to anger; but bring them up in the discipline and instruction of the Lord.

— Ephesians 6:1-4

Parenthood brings much joy, but also much responsibility. By understanding how demons operate, parents can shield their children from their attacks and from their bindings. If spirits get a foothold, it is the parents' responsibility, especially for younger children, to step in and take back the ground they have gained.

The husband and wife are to provide an atmosphere of love and security for the family, keeping the home free from negative tensions. Although Shirley was one of eleven children, she never once heard her parents argue or criticize others. She has since learned that they dealt with their differences privately, so that the children lived in a strife-free and restful environment.

Fathers need to realize that a child's image of the heavenly Father is being moulded on their own father role in the home. If a child only knows a father who is angry, abusive, cruel, and indifferent, it can be hard to comprehend a heavenly Father who is loving and kind. If children grow up with years of disrespect for an earthly father, they may not readily be able to respond to a heavenly Father.

Prevention is better than cure — so the saying goes. Children are to be trained in the ways of the Lord and encouraged to develop a vital, personal relationship with Him. As they learn to walk in obedience to God's Word and are encouraged to continually choose the way of righteousness, they are automatically protected from many of the enemy's wiles. Also firm and loving discipline needs to be given when required.

How important that parents choose carefully the words they speak to their children. We prayed for a married man who was bound by spirits of failure and rejection. For years his father had kept telling him he was no good and would never amount to anything. Evil spirits thrive in such an atmosphere, and build up their holds in little lives through "words." Speak words that edify, not words that tear down.

Parents should also be sensitive to needs a child may have. Johnny may come home from school feeling rejected and inferior because other children were calling him names. Comfort him, encourage him to have the right response to those who have hurt him, and pray with him claiming freedom from any effect or inroad of the enemy.

Children can easily grasp the realities of spiritual conflict, and should be taught how they can do their part to keep themselves walking closely with Jesus. But it is imperative that these truths be shared in wisdom so that there is no ground given for any fear of the enemy. The reality of Jesus being Lord and Satan being defeated must be imparted. Continually center their attention on the love, power, and glory of the Lord Jesus Christ. Let them grow up Christ-conscious.

Praying for children is sometimes best done when they are awake, and sometimes best done when they are asleep.

If you pray for a child when he is awake, it should be done with the child's cooperation. Choose the right time: a time when the child is not overactive. You can sit small children on your lap.

As you are ministering, there can be various reactions: the child may sit quietly and feel nothing happening; he may become tired and go to sleep (don't stop praying if he does); he may become restless and uncooperative and perhaps want to run away.

A few days ago we were praying for a very young child that began to cry and cry. My natural reaction was to stop and let the mother bring comfort. However, we were aware that the source of the agitation was spirits that were manifesting and trying to divert us from praying. We therefore continued praying until we felt led to stop. The child settled down to a good night's sleep and was noticeably changed the next day.

It is not always necessary to use the words "evil spirits." If you are coming against spirits of rejection, simply say: "We come against this hold of rejection in Jesus' name. Rejection, we bind you and break your hold in the name of Jesus. . . ."

If when a child is awake, he is too restless, or will not

cooperate, or has difficulty with rebellion, then it is best to pray for him when he is asleep. Remember, however, that whatever you say in his presence will go into his mind. It is not a good idea to go into his room and have a discussion about him before you begin to pray.

Lay your hands on the child and speak quietly against the enemy. Again be positive in your words. Initially you can name the area or areas in which you are claiming release, but from then on, you can generalize. If the problem is rebellion, you could say: "Spirits of rebellion, we command *you* in Jesus' name to go with his breath. We loose him into *obedience*. We set his mind and will free from *these pressures*. Every *band* is broken. There is no place for *your* grip. You have been named and we break your *pressures* now. . . ."

It is also good to quote verses of Scripture that are applicable to the area of need. This is positive truth going down into his mind even though he is asleep.

When you first recognize the need to set your children free, you may find it best to minister to them regularly every day or every week for a certain period of time. It may be a short time or a long time. Learn to be guided by the Holy Spirit as to when you should conclude. As you look to Him, you can develop an awareness within as to when to keep praying and when to stop.

Adopted children usually need deliverance in areas such as rejection and insecurity.

A lovely Christian couple brought their nine-year-old adopted son for prayer. The boy knew the Lord and wanted to follow Him closely, but for some months had been very rebellious. Not only were the parents upset, but he was too. He did not want to be this way. Unknown to him, his real mother had been a rebellious young teenager when she gave birth to him. Spirits of rebellion had been transferred from mother to son in the womb, and now they were seeking to manifest their presence. Together we came against spirits of rebellion and other areas that the Lord impressed us to speak against. The dear young boy has been changed since that time.

When spirits of rebellion are driven out of children, they are free to willingly obey. Of course they also need instruction to see the importance of obedience, and they must desire in their heart to walk in obedience. We have seen many parents thrilled with the changes in the attitudes and responses of their children as they have been set free.

As we minister to our children in dependence upon the Lord Jesus, we will discover the reality of a living and caring Christ. How real will be our faith in Him and how precious He will be to us.

Chapter 19

Questions and Answers on Deliverance

1. Who should be involved in ministering deliverance?

Every believer can be involved in self-deliverance, and also every believer should come to a place where he knows how to pray for others if called upon. Not all will major in this ministry. There will be particular people whom the Lord will raise up and equip to specialize. It is to be anticipated that those who are ministry gifts to the Body, especially evangelists, will move in this realm.

Praying for others is not a realm for the immature or novice. We must first know how our enemy operates and how to keep ourselves in the midst of warfare. To be uninformed is to be vulnerable.

2. Should deliverance be ministered privately or publicly?

Jesus set people free in both public and private places. We have to be willing to deal with the need where and when it occurs. Some people are afraid to have unusual things happening in their services, that break into the years of "respectable tradition." Let us be open to the Holy Spirit and learn to flow with what He desires to do — whether it be in public or private.

Many people request private counsel. This is helpful when the person has deep needs he wishes to share. There are many needs, however, that can be met in a public meeting.

If there are individuals who, through demonic manifestations, regularly distract the flow of meetings (such as the Sunday worship service), then it is good to take them aside and deal with them privately.

3. What place do public deliverance meetings have?

They have a very important place. The preaching of the Word

should not be separated from signs (healing and deliverance) following:

> *And Philip went down to the city of Samaria and began proclaiming Christ to them. And the multitudes with one accord were giving attention to what was said by Philip, as they heard and saw the signs which he was performing. For in the case of many who had unclean spirits, they were coming out of them shouting with a loud voice; and many who had been paralyzed and lame were healed.*
>
> — *Acts 8:5-7*

The needs of people within and without the church are so great they cannot be met by a pastor here or a counselor there. By gathering people in need together for special services, the Word can be preached, instruction given, and faith released. In an atmosphere like this, great things can happen as the Lord Jesus moves in confirming signs.

My own involvement in deliverance meetings came because I did not have the time to pray individually for all who were seeking counsel. A fellow minister suggested we should gather together those who were needing prayer and deal with them en masse. So began regular meetings in which about forty-five minutes of teaching led into an hour or more of mass prayer and deliverance as the Holy Spirit guided. The emphasis of the meetings was to teach people to release their faith and receive self-deliverance rather than have them dependent on a counselor.

4. Should I pray for deliverance for people of the opposite sex?

Under normal circumstances, this is not advisable. It is preferable for men to pray for men, and women for women. When it is not possible, it is important that you have with you another counselor of the same sex as the counselee. I always try to have a woman counselor with me when praying for women. No suspicion must be given by unwise actions. By having a witness, the counselor is protected from any false accusations of improper conduct. We must be a step ahead of Satan who will try to do anything he can to hinder a legitimate ministry. If a man is praying alone for a woman and demons are manifesting with loud cries, it may be hard to convince a bypasser, who does not understand this realm, that everything is in order. Be wise.

5. Do you recommend counseling teams?

Certainly, provided the teams have good counselors.

In a private counseling time, I personally would not want more than five people praying for one person. If others were involved, I would have them interceding in a nearby location with communication kept between the two groups. It can be overwhelming for the counselee if too many counselors are involved. I normally work with only one other counselor.

A counseling team provides opportunity for new workers to gain experience by working alongside seasoned counselors.

A husband and wife team can be very effective.

6. Should you attempt to minister deliverance to someone who doesn't want you to?

You cannot force yourself on people no matter how concerned you may feel for them. Before a believer can begin to receive deliverance, he must consent to it.

Some people are frightened or unwilling to acknowledge that they need help. In these cases, it is best to wait until they become really desperate and open to receive ministry. In the meantime, you can in your own prayer times take authority over the spirits that are hindering their right responses and intercede for them as the Holy Spirit directs you.

Occasionally a counselee will rise up and spirits will speak through him saying things such as: "I'm getting out of here." "You're not going to pray for me again." "I hate you." "Leave me alone." When these demonic manifestations occur, you need to recognize them as such and firmly tell the person not to consent to the manifestations, but to cooperate with you as you command the spirits to go.

7. Can I pray for someone's deliverance when separated by distance?

Yes, you can pray for a person to be set free although he is in another location. Distance is no barrier to the Holy Spirit. Do we not pray for our missionary friends and believe God to honor our prayers, even though they may be far away?

The keys when praying for someone are that you are led by the Holy Spirit and that you release faith as you pray.

8. Can an unconverted person be set free?

Generally speaking a person needs to come to Jesus as Savior and Lord before deliverance can be received.

Unbelievers may sometimes receive a measure of deliverance as a sign to them of God's love and power. Many will then turn and give their lives to Christ.

In Acts 28:7-9 we read of Paul ministering to unbelievers when he was shipwrecked on Malta. Publius, the leading man of the island, had given hospitality to Paul and those with him. When Paul learned that Publius' father was very sick, he prayed and laid his hands on him, and he was healed. The news spread and the rest of the people on the island who were sick also came to Paul to be healed.

To minister to unbelievers in this way is a glorious opportunity to witness to the reality and power of Jesus Christ; to say that what happens when you pray is happening because Jesus is touching them; and to encourage them to open their hearts to Him. However, there is no guarantee that what God does for them will remain if they afterwards choose to reject His way.

9. Is it right to converse with demons and ask them their names?

With the exception of occasionally asking a spirit its name, we should stay away from conversations with demons. I say this for two reasons:

First, because evil spirits are wicked beings that cannot be trusted. They will lie and deceive you. Even when asked their names, they may or may not tell the truth. There is a story which goes:

Counselor: "Evil spirit, what is your name?"

Spirit: "I'm a lying spirit."

Counselor: "Are you telling the truth?"

Identifying spirits can be helpful in getting them out. When revealed by name, there is a weakening of their hold. However, there is only one recorded incident in the Bible in which a spirit was asked its name. The reply was "Legion" (Mark 5:9) which was more a statement of how many demons there were, rather than a declaration of what kind they were. We should approach the matter of asking demons their names with caution. I do it myself only on rare occasions, preferring to rely on discernment from the Holy Spirit.

When spirits are asked their names, sometimes they answer through the person's mouth (some will lie), and sometimes there is no response. When there is no response, it may be that the person is so resisting the spirits, that they cannot find expression through his lips. You could try asking the person to say what is being said in his mind. He may say that he hears the word "self-hate" repeating itself. Name this area and command release.

The second reason why it is not good to converse with evil spirits, is that it comes very close to the practice of a medium, which is communicating with evil spirits. This practice is forbidden in Scripture. Deuteronomy 18:10-12.

Christians do not need to consult evil spirits to get information. The Holy Spirit is our source. Through the gifts of discernings of spirits and the word of knowledge, the Holy Spirit can tell us the names of spirits and anything else we need to know about the area of bondage.

10. Is there a distinction between the works of the flesh and the works of demons?

Although the two are closely linked, there is a difference. Galatians 5:19-21 gives a list of works of the flesh which include immorality, sensuality, sorcery, jealousy, outbursts of anger, drunkenness, and so on. These are deeds that proceed from those areas of man's nature which are not under the control of the Holy Spirit. If we constantly give ourselves to works of the flesh, we open ourselves to demonic infiltration in the areas we yield to. For example, a person who regularly gives place to immorality will open himself to spirits of immorality. The bondage area may begin in the flesh, but then be strengthened by the entrance of evil spirits.

11. Is there a relationship between the "healing of memories" and deliverance?

Yes, there is. The "healing of memories" is the bringing of deliverance to people in a "low-key" way. Many who minister "healing of memories" or "inner healing" would not realize that they are actually ministering deliverance from demons; yet this is what is happening. Inner healing is certainly taking place; for inner healing, or harmony, comes when demons are cast out.

Because "healing of memories" is not a scriptural term, I personally do not use it.

12. When a spirit is cast out, is there a danger that it may enter someone else nearby?

Yes, there is a possibility, and for this reason I always claim protection upon others who may be nearby. If praying for someone in their own home, I claim protection upon every family member. Faith overcomes fear. We must see our victory and the enemy's defeat. The spirits are the ones who are afraid and on the run — not ourselves. We are to be bold and fearless in Christ.

Because of my personal faith in Christ's power to keep and deliver, I never fear babies or children being present — even in public deliverance meetings. I welcome their presence knowing that they will be blessed, rather than harmed, in a gathering where the Holy Spirit is moving in power. It all hinges on our faith.

On the other hand, a person who is closed to the Holy Spirit's ministry and expressing disdain and mockery at people being delivered could become a target for spirits that have just left others.

13. If a person exercises spiritual gifts, does that mean he is completely free of all bondage?

Certainly not. God does not wait until we are free from all bondage before He works through us. A person, for example, may have a healing ministry with gifts of healings operating through him, and yet have areas of his life that still need to be cleansed. The operation of a spiritual gift in great power is not necessarily an indication of a life totally free from all bondage.

14. Is there a need for homes or buildings to be cleansed?

As spirits can linger in homes, or around or in objects with which they have been associated, there often needs to be a cleansing.

It is not difficult to cleanse a home. The believing occupants should come together and consciously yield the home or property to the Lord, bind the workings of evil spirits in Jesus' name, and then declare the dwelling sanctified because of the power of the blood of Jesus Christ. When I do this, I go from room to room declaring cleansing in Jesus' name. You may even desire to walk into the grounds and declare that the dwelling and land are the Lord's property. When moving into a new home, if we feel it necessary, the first thing Shirley and I do is cleanse it. We certainly always dedicate it to God.

A friend of mine was pastoring a church that began renting a former picture theatre for their services. In the theatre there was such a coldness in the atmosphere that people commented on it. The elders, on considering it, became aware of a demonic presence. They fasted and then went through the building claiming release. My friend was absent at the time, but on returning walked alone through the building and sensed the cleansing was not complete. Twice he walked into the men's washrooms and twice the hair on the back of his neck stood on end. The Lord revealed to him the presence of spirits of homosexuality which he then commanded to leave in Jesus' name. He continued to rebuke until he felt the building cleansed. The following

178

Sunday, the people, without knowing what the elders had done, commented on the warmth in the building and how the coldness had gone. The power of Satan had been broken.

15. Can everyone minister self-deliverance?

The majority of believers can, but there are always some who lack the strength of character or who have some lack mentally, and are themselves unable to rise up. Others need to take the initiative to minister to those who are "genuinely" weak.

Through experience we have discovered that some believers initially need help from others to get underway, even though they understand the principles of self-deliverance. The counselor must discern when the person can carry on himself and no longer needs to lean on others.

There can be times when a person who has successfully ministered much self-deliverance, comes to a place where he needs help from someone else for a short period.

16. Can children practice self-deliverance?

Most certainly children can practice self-deliverance. I know children of varying ages who are able to cooperate with the Lord and bring themselves deliverance.

With younger children, it should be the parents who take the responsibility to minister to them. As they become older, they can be more independent.

Don't underestimate the capacity of children in spiritual understanding. They often grasp spiritual principles more quickly than adults.

17. Should parents be present when a child is being counseled for deliverance?

Yes, if possible both parents should be with their child. In the New Testament, we read of parents bringing their children to Jesus (Mark 7:25-30; Matthew 17:14-21). Because parents have the responsibility under God for the instruction and nurturing of their children, it is important they are there.

When I have parents present, I teach them how to pray for the child. Although I take the initiative and do most of the praying, I also encourage them to spend a time praying and so learn to minister by doing.

18. I don't feel victorious and I don't feel I have any authority to set myself free. What should I do?

The deciding issue is not what you feel like, but what God's Word declares. Identified with Christ, you share His victory and triumph over the enemy. Start thanking God by faith for the victory you have in Christ. Commence the principles of self-deliverance, regardless of how you feel.

19. I have tried to release myself, but nothing seems to happen.

Make sure the ingredient of "faith" is in operation. If as you come against strongholds, you believe that what you say is happening, there will be a measure of weakening and breaking — even if you don't feel it. Perhaps more perseverance is required before you will feel any changes. If, after some time (weeks or months), you are still perturbed, seek an understanding counselor who can pray with you and release you into a place where things are obviously happening. Some people need encouragement to help them start the pathway to deliverance.

20. How will I know when I am completely free?

It is the responsibility of the Holy Spirit to bear witness to you of your complete freedom.

Sometimes I confidently declare to a person that a certain area of bondage is completely broken; but I only do this if I know by the Spirit that it is so. Very often, even after a great deliverance, I tell the person that God has a further work to do in that same area. Untold damage is done when counselors incorrectly tell people they are free.

It is usually quite easy for a person to know if he has had at least a measure of deliverance. The reactions and stirrings will have gone and there will be a feeling of freedom. Some may not feel anything immediately, but will notice evidence of it in the coming days. Sometimes people get free, but do not realize it. With the problem gone, they easily forget about it. It is not until something reminds them of how they used to be, that they realize they are changed. How careful we should be not to forget what God has done for us and to give Him thanks.

Often people "feel" they are completely free from a problem area, but discover months or even years later that more release is needed. It is not because they have been re-bound, but because the Holy Spirit is reaching down to root out further depths of satanic inroads in their lives. When a major deliverance takes place, remaining spirits in the family may lie low, not manifesting for fear of also being exposed and cast out. Although the person feels free, he often needs much more deliverance. I believe God allows us to enjoy measures of release before entering new battles, so that we are not having extended periods of heavy warfare without a break.

Let us major on the Lord Jesus and constantly declare our completeness in Him. This will release His power to bring to light areas that need to be dealt with. Major on the faith confession that you *are* free; not on the hope confession that one day you *will be* free.

Chapter 20

Personal Testimonies

While a member of a pastoral team in Australia, it was my privilege to counsel many people and teach them the ways of self-deliverance. In this chapter are testimonies from a number of these people, both men and women, most of whom are very well known to us. We are grateful to them for sharing their experiences and to others who took time to write, but have not had their stories included. All are responsible and dedicated Christians and would typify a cross section of believers in any local church community.

Although most were happy for us to use their names, we thought it best for their testimonies to be anonymous. An exception was made in the final testimony which is by Daphne Drummond who was my able assistant in many a counseling session.

As you read of the delivering power of Jesus in the lives of others, may you be encouraged to reach out in faith and believe God for your own freedom.

"I found myself exploding with rage."

1976 was a year of adventure and growth! God led me into full-time missionary work that year, calling me from Australia to New Zealand, Indonesia, Singapore, and Malaysia. Consequently, when my church asked me to begin a new Bible School in the jungles of Papua New Guinea, I anticipated yet further delightful years of happy service. But God had higher plans. He wasn't calling me to an extended holiday, but to growth. God seems more interested in character than comfort and the years ahead were to be full of valuable lessons learned at a price. It is of one of these lessons that I now wish to write. . . .

Our first group of twenty-three students was wonderful. They were lively individuals eager to learn and quick to communicate. But as the months went by, deep flaws began to appear in both their characters and mine. Some of the boys had recurring lust problems;

183

there was an habitual liar; one boy was still involved in magic; and I found myself exploding in rage at times in the classroom.

The second intake was not of the same caliber as the first. In short, I found them more challenging and at times more irritating. One lad couldn't look at anyone in the face, but constantly hit his forehead with his hand and stammered badly when speaking. Another refused to speak. Yet another ran away and got drunk, while a fourth had such trouble with violence that I was afraid to be near him. And my own problem with anger only grew worse.

One morning at six, smoke began to rise from a cooking fire in the school gardens below. I grew hot with fury. There was a strict rule that no one did any cooking during this hour's quiet-time. Not wanting to respond out of anger, I turned my eyes away from the telltale spiral of smoke and tried to pray. But my anger grew hotter and hotter. Nothing succeeded in taking my mind from that smoke. Finally the dam burst, and I rushed madly down the steps into the garden house. Four startled girl students saw me in time and scrambled into the tapioca bushes. Sweeping up a log, I surged into the shelter smashing pots and lids, scattering rice, bananas, and coals in my wake. The student body was furious with my actions and terrible currents of hate ran through the school that day.

God is good. I repented and apologized, and the students forgave. But my problem had become a little too obvious.

Finally came end-of-year holidays and a much needed rest in Australia. Also, finally we heard Pastor Powell minister on freedom from evil spirits. Words can't express my relief when I embraced this new hope. Prayer, fasting, self-control, positive confession had all helped clean up areas of sin in my life; but some areas remained seemingly immovable, until this pastor prayed with me for deliverance.

Amazingly, Pastor Powell didn't pray against the spirits of anger in me, but he did teach me to warfare daily for my own release from three other major strongholds. Each morning in my quiet-time, after meditating on the Bible, a time of vocal warfare would follow. Spirits left my body, manifesting their departure in deep yawning and burping.

Some months went by. We were back in the Bible School with a new group of students. But a wondrous thing had happened. No anger. Often confronted with situations that would have turned my insides to fire a year earlier, I was astonished to find peace. There was

184

no struggle to attain this peace, for when all the spirits were gone, all the symptoms were gone too.

Enthusiastically we taught the students the principles of deliverance I had learned from Pastor Powell. For more than a month we had daily Bible teaching and group prayer on the subject. The results were beyond our highest hopes. We had previously called certain problems "personality disorders." Now it became apparent that many disorders were rooted in evil spirits. For example, the boy who constantly hit his head had returned to repeat the course. In a month he had received so much deliverance that he was freed into being a delightful person and grew to be the brightest student of all. The demons of shame and shyness left him. Confusion, insanity, and a family curse which had been passed down through generations had kept this boy bound. Prayer in Jesus' name had now bound those spirits and cast them out. Wonderfully, that student was released and immediately began to evangelize! From being the most shy student, he became the boldest witness for the Lord Jesus. We staff felt so sorry that we had taken one and a half years to help this boy, but we praised God that it wasn't too late.

Every student benefited. One young man had once discovered the dead body of a friend drowned in a river. The dreadful shock had left its mark. When we began to bind the spirit of fear, the young man went into shock again. The battle against these spirits went on for some months, but the resulting freedom was well worth it.

The student who refused to speak grasped the truth of deliverance. Every morning we could hear him praising God out in the jungle and warfaring against demons in himself. After weeks of wholehearted struggle we saw him blossom into a precious preacher of God's Word. Strangely enough, we noticed that the area of previous bondage often afterwards became one of the strongest areas of the person's personality.

Of course, deliverance was not the magic word that cleared up all problems in a month. We continued weekly ministry all year and saw more release, although many problems were not demon-based and had to be dealt with in the other tried scriptural ways.

Since that time, each new body of students has experienced glorious releases, adding more and more evidence for the place and beauty of the deliverance ministry in the normal Christian life.

"I was very self-destructive and frequently suicidal."

Before I became a Christian, I suffered premenstrual tension

185

and depression to such an extent that for twenty-four hours each month I was completely unable to cope with life. Predictable as it was, I was never able to see that the depression would pass. Each time I would go into such depression that I felt I wouldn't live through it. I was very self-destructive and frequently suicidal.

My husband could never understand how a seemingly logical and coherent adult could almost in an instant become so unglued. Situations which one day looked acceptable, the very next day, were unbearable. Of course this changeability caused rifts in our marriage. My husband felt sorry for me to a certain extent in that I was so desperately unhappy, and often felt very concerned for my safety, sometimes even staying up most of the night to ensure I didn't run off or kill myself.

When I became a Christian, I gained a substantial degree of control over myself — much to the joy of my husband and children. I then became pregnant and had my third child. Postnatal depression was for the first time a real problem, and despite growing faith in Christ, I was unable to walk one day in victory over depression and resentment. I confided in a woman at church; I really feel God led me to share with her as she was able to minister to me in a way that very few others could have done at that time.

She suggested that the problem was likely demonic in origin. I was ready to give anything a try and gladly agreed when she offered to come and pray for me at home. The next day as we prayed I was delivered. I felt the spirits going and experienced a mild sort of physical discomfort as they went. I was so elated. I hadn't felt so free from heaviness for months. I was a bit skeptical when it was suggested that I might need more deliverance. Over the following months I was delivered of many, many evil spirits.

I began to learn to pray for my own freedom, to command an area such as fear or infirmity to leave, and to keep pressure on until I experienced release. The actual time varied from a few minutes to days, and in some areas I haven't yet come to experience that real freedom. Many times I found it necessary to get help from others whose faith and persistence were more developed than my own.

For eighteen months now I have been free of that inevitable plunge into depression each month. I have, since I learned the principles of deliverance, experienced an increasing freedom in my personality. I have come into a joy and peace that I never would have believed possible for me.

"A spirit of death was upon my unborn baby."

May 1979 found me expecting our second child. Of course my husband and I were thrilled, but deep inside me was a nagging thought that all was far from well with this new life God was entrusting to us. For months I was to know the agony of pain and heavy bleeding. Complete bed rest in hospital and then at home was ordered by my specialist. The feelings inside grew into a deep fear that my baby would die before the full term of pregnancy; would be stillborn; or even worse, would live, but be severely handicapped.

My doctors (I had three on my case) all agreed I had a full placenta previa. This is when the afterbirth or placenta is below the baby instead of above. The weight of the baby presses on the placenta and forces it down into the neck of the womb and a tear occurs and bleeding and pain follows. This is dangerous as the bleeding can't be stopped and the unborn baby could die in fifteen minutes. The mother also suffers from shock which can be serious. I was living on a tightrope. At any moment I could have a massive hemorrhage and my baby would be dead! I cried out to God, but felt He had abandoned me. But His timing wasn't my timing, nor His plans, my plans.

One weekend Graham and Shirley Powell, whom I knew quite well, ministered at my church, but being confined to bed, I couldn't attend any of their deliverance meetings; so they came to me. I was thirty-five weeks pregnant and had only felt my baby moving slightly. The doctors couldn't detect a heartbeat unless they used an ultrasonic machine. They had prepared me for the worst. Graham and Shirley talked with me and I shared my deep fears. Graham sensed that a spirit of death was upon my unborn baby. A wonderful calm came over me as they prayed, loosed that foul spirit, and then ministered to the baby. For the first time the baby moved forcefully inside me and from that day on the baby's movements could be felt quite definitely. We were set free!

When my doctor came to examine me a few days later, he said I could try staying out of bed for short periods of time. Without knowing it, he confirmed what God had already done: set me free. I'm an active person; so those long seven months in bed were almost too much to endure.

On January 10, 1980 by Caesarean section I gave birth to a baby girl. She weighed nine pounds five ounces, a miracle in itself as the doctors had told us to expect only a four-to-five-pound baby, because of all the bleeding. We named her Tamarah, which means "like a palm tree." *Palm* means "victory," and Tamarah is a mighty victory in God. She is a constant reminder to us that Christ did more than die for our sins; His very life brings us deliverance and healing.

"I spent seven years in mental hospitals."

My life has changed so much in the last few months, it's been astounding. After seven years of black depressions, nightmares, hallucinations, and all kinds of hideous changes in my personality, I am relieved to know the problem has been demonic and not some terrible mental illness. I spent seven years in public mental hospitals and expensive private hospitals under all kinds of treatments, drugs and therapies, with no improvement. Like most other patients I kept coming back and getting worse. Just before I got saved, I was in a mental home, and they said they were just waiting for me to crack completely. They wanted to put me in a locked ward for my own protection. I was rapidly losing weight, having severe chest pains, and my stomach was ulcerated. My body temperature went down, and I was always cold. I couldn't sleep at night because of nightmares and hallucinations, and I could barely talk. The doctors said I had a depressive personality disorder, or I was a paranoid schizophrenic, or other labels.

The most wonderful night of my life was when I asked the Lord to wash away my sins and come into my heart. For the first time I felt clean, and I had peace and joy that I had never known. But in the months that followed the attacks continued. My mind had a tight band around it, and headaches, and often a burning sensation, and blurred vision, and extreme confusion. My chest used to feel as if it had a ton of weight in it, and I had acute tension and often trembling and nervousness. I felt bound in my personality. I couldn't be myself, and had strong feelings of inferiority, and a horrible feeling within myself that I couldn't describe. When I was around people, I was extremely tense and jumpy and couldn't sit still, and was constantly attention-seeking although I didn't want to. I often went out on altar calls for prayer, but with no results. However, I was confident God would make me whole again.

The second greatest moment of my life was when I discovered that my problems were caused by demons and not myself. Through seeing Graham Powell and hearing his tapes, I learned that I had the victory and authority over demons and that they were defeated at the Cross. In the world your hope diminishes, but with the Lord the light grows brighter and brighter. I learned about spiritual warfare and that

I had weapons and armor that were mighty through God. All this was exciting, and for the first time in my life I wasn't bowed down under defeat, but rising up to conquer.

The changes in my life have been astounding. I was always paralyzed with all kinds of fears. I couldn't talk to people. I would shake and sweat and have palpitations and all kinds of horrible physical reactions to many fears. Now through using my spiritual weapons, God has delivered me from fear and I have a new self-confidence. I am making new friends, going out to meetings and giving testimonies, praying for others, and doing all kinds of things I was incapable of doing before. I used to be locked in my own house, terrified that someone would come to the door.

God has also set me free from fear of failure and insecurity, and my marriage has had a healing. My husband and I are sharing a new love, and our house is filled with a new joy and presence of the Lord. Before, I was so insecure that I would be crying or depressed or quarreling and attacking my husband. Also since I've been delivered from inferiority, I am confident as a wife and mother and as a person. I have become close to my husband's family recently because I am confident of sharing myself again. I feel like a worthwhile person. Before I had shut them off.

I don't have black depressions or hallucinations any more, and God has healed my stomach from ulcers and my brain from the effects of overdoses. Also I am not skinny any more. The Lord also delivered me from the spirit of loneliness. I used to feel alone even in a crowd, but now I am living happily on a farm and don't feel any loneliness.

There have been so many changes, and only in a few months. Through spiritual warfare God has given me strength and peace to cover my heart and my mind, and I am looking forward to life each day instead of dreading it.

"I was cursed by people who hated me."

As missionaries, we sometimes become careless and complacent, not acknowledging our moment by moment need of protection from dark, evil powers around us.

At one gloomy time, I was cursed by people who hated me because I stood with those who turned their backs on funeral feasts that were full of heathen practices.

Another time, I was in a place where I was often in contact with a man possessed by evil spirits. I asked others to help me to pray for him, but they all refused because they said when they prayed for him they always became sick. Nylon cords binding his wrists had caused huge infected sores which I treated for him. When they were almost healed he asked me for my hand. I thought he wanted to shake hands to express gratitude, but he pulled my fingers and sent spirits into me. I cried out to God and pulled my hand free, but the encounter was more serious than I had realized.

For most of my missionary career (28 years), I had suffered from tropical fevers and weakness, strong fears, and sometimes depressions. Some of the fevers and other symptoms were ordinary, but many were a puzzle to doctors.

After being delivered from curses, spirits of death, suicide, infirmity, loneliness, inferiority, discouragement, disappointment and many other things, I found that my life has really changed. I have had only one day's sickness in the past eighteen months which is remarkable. I have a new confidence in the Lord Jesus Christ which enables me to cope boldly with the situations that arise, even confrontations that I would normally seek to escape from. It is true that if Jesus makes us free, then we are free indeed (John 8:36).

"I retreated into a complete fantasy world."

I came to know the Lord Jesus Christ at the age of twenty-four during the final year of a university course. Although I was raised in an environment where I came to know God in a childlike way, during my teen years I turned my back on the principles of God and went my own way. This led to years of heavy involvement in drugs and alcohol which left my personality in a shattered state, to say the least. I had grown up with an over-riding feeling of inferiority and insecurity. I felt an incredible need to prove myself to others; to be something in the eyes of men. During my years of drug dependence, these problems magnified themselves, as well as many others appearing.

On coming to Christ, I found a wonderful release from many burdens and problems that had bound me. A depression that had hung over my life for years lifted, never to return. However, as I moved on with God, many of the old problems began to manifest; and in many cases, in an increasing measure. My first realization that these were caused by demonic forces, came when I was being ministered to at a youth camp. There came a stirring from within, and to my amazement, I began screaming uncontrollably. I experienced a wonderful release from inferiority, and in the days that followed I noticed real changes within me.

This was the beginning of a period of deliverance which was to last for two years. At times it was difficult as the works of darkness manifested in my life. I experienced times of sheer torment and feelings of complete unreality as if I were going out of my mind. At the same time I was pressing on with God with all my heart. It amazed me the extent to which negative emotions began to manifest: feelings of loneliness, rejection, inferiority, fears, to name a few. However, as the enemy manifested, the Lord brought deliverance both when others ministered to me and as I prayed against the enemy myself. Such was the extent of deliverance, that many times I began to doubt whether the problems were really caused by evil spirits. However, time and time again, I found release leading to changes in my daily life.

One particular area in which the enemy had built strongholds into my personality was in my mind. As a teenager in high school, I found study difficult in terms of concentration. I chose during those years to rebel against the discipline of my parents and to give in to lazy idle ways which were increasingly reflected in an undisciplined mind. My involvement with drugs greatly magnified the problem to the extent that I retreated into a complete fantasy world. My university study was a frustration because I found it difficult to concentrate for more than five minutes at a time.

On coming to know the Lord, I noticed definite changes in this area as I began to soak in the Word of God. For the first year of my Christian life I left my studies and worked as a gardener. This relieved much of the pressure and it enhanced God's renewal process. However, on returning to my studies, I found the old problem of mental distraction still with me. As a Christian, it was even more a problem because my desire to succeed was much greater, and hence there was a frustration and sense of defeat which the enemy would bring upon me. I also began to find it difficult to concentrate on study of the Word. I found also I had to battle with impurity in my mind, however much I detested this and desired to be righteous in the sight of God.

I found mental discipline one of the most difficult areas to get victory in. It took a long time before I even recognized a need for deliverance in this area. I thought that if I saturated my mind with the Word of God, then I would find freedom in my mind. But when concentration on the Word was difficult, this presented a problem. When I recognized my need for deliverance and battled with the enemy — sometimes with the aid of fasting — then a soundness of mind gradually came. I began to be able to take in God's Word to

191

allow it to do its renewal process. While undergoing deliverance from these mental bondages, God also challenged me on the need to build disciplined patterns into my daily life.

I came to realize that perseverance was vital to achieving total release from the enemy's strongholds. Also I came to realize that I had to take up the weapons that God had provided and bring my own release, rather than all the time depending on a counselor. I found that if I lingered in prayer in a certain area (sometimes up to an hour or more) then the chains began to break from my personality. As I began to take up the fight myself, I found I had a greater measure of control over the enemy's manifestations; I no longer had the dramatic manifestations of earlier deliverances.

I also discovered that the enemy tried everything he could to hinder my deliverance. Often thoughts such as, "You are being selfish praying for yourself all the time," would spring into my mind when I sensed warfare was necessary. However, as the years have gone by, and as I have rejected these enemy influences, I have come to experience the liberty of Calvary in a very real sense in my life.

"I was convinced my problems were just me."

When I was a child, my parents quarreled bitterly. I vividly remember scenes when Mum locked Dad out of the house and then locked us all into the main bedroom, hammering it securely with nails in case he broke in. I often lay awake at night, listening for his return and planning how to protect the younger children if he grew violent. Although I was an outwardly obedient child, deep roots of fear, rebellion, and disrespect for authority were establishing themselves in my life.

I longed desperately for affection, but my parents were too bound to be able to express it. I found acceptance only in accomplishment at school, but this failed to satisfy the hunger in my heart. I wanted to talk deeply and freely to my parents, but found they were not able to receive my confidences.

I became a Christian at seventeen, and the following year attended a short-term Bible college. But as time went on, I became conscious of deep bondages in my life. I had such a problem with embarrassment and fear that at times my voice would tighten with apprehension and sound strange; and at really bad times, my mouth moved at the corner. I blushed deeply and often, and hated myself for doing it. I found it difficult to express myself in group situations. I longed to be myself, and to be free to communicate and live in the way that I felt was "me." My dream life was also very disturbed.

Although I praised God, confessed His Word, attended church and church activities, and had regular quiet times, I could find no answers. I tried every spiritual and psychological thing I could think of, but nothing worked.

Then some of my friends began to find answers through deliverance. I looked on with longing, thinking how fortunate they were to be set free in that way. For myself, I was convinced that my problems were just me, and that I would have them for the rest of my life.

God is merciful, however, and there came a time when I moved into a house with people involved in the ministry of deliverance. I acknowledged my need, and a process began that has continued for over two years.

As I pressed into deliverance, I noticed some dramatic changes taking place. The nightmares ceased; deep-rooted bondages began to go; I found myself expressing myself in group situations and in prayer; and a new freedom came in my relationships with people.

At different stages, I have been so delighted with the new measure of freedom that I had found that I could almost have settled for that measure. But I knew I must press on further.

I praise God for His mighty delivering power. I am amazed how He can take a life and transform it in the depths of personality. I feel like a sailing boat that has been moored at a desert island, with many anchors hanging down preventing it from moving out to sea. I am now stepping out in new areas, and becoming more and more free to move with the Holy Spirit, acting in obedience to His commands, and flowing with Him — like a sailing boat that is loosed from the shore lines and skims out over deep waters.

"I had been a drug addict . . . deeply involved in the occult."

Before becoming a Christian, I had been a drug addict for many years, and deeply involved in the occult. I had come from a home which had been broken by suicide, immorality, and bitterness.

During the first six years of my Christian life, under God's conviction, my life was "cleaned up" and changed. There were many problems in my life, but I had developed a close relationship with Jesus and come off drugs, and I expected that my problems would continue to disappear. Everything seemed to be progressing well, but there were difficulties I could not overcome, no matter how much I

193

prayed, fasted, and sought God. I had had some deliverance as a young Christian, and had been told I did not need any more.

The main problems that concerned me were:

(a) Severe pressure, tension, and anxiety which had so gripped me in my new teaching position that for several months, I had been unable to relax, even in the presence of God.

(b) I found to my distress that the more I sought God, nearly every time He manifested His presence in a powerful way, my head would feel as if it were about to blow apart, and a band of tension would so grip me that my jaw clenched and parts of my body became rigid.

(c) I had become alarmed that the unusual number of accidents and mishaps in my life had not ceased. I was aware that these attacks (car accidents, being attacked, near drowning, etc.) were from a satanic source, but could not understand why they continued despite my Christian commitment.

There were other things I was less desperate about, problems I had become used to as "part of my personality" or "a result of my past." These included innumerable fears, feelings of rejection despite my many friends, persistent insomnia, nervous symptoms that were often crippling both physically and emotionally, and an over-susceptibility to illness.

I sought God, and becoming desperate for an answer, went to see Graham Powell. He realized that my problems were demonic and told me so. I was reluctant to accept it at first, but the immediate release from pressure and anxiety resulting from his prayers made me keen to follow this way of dealing with the problems. Many sessions of prayer and counseling followed, often with demons manifesting violently, sometimes with little manifestation.

The results have been marked: I now rarely get sick. I sleep well. Feelings of rejection no longer cripple my personality. Whereas once my underlying feelings in every relationship were: does he or she accept me? I am now able to be less self-centered and give love and acceptance to others.

Some areas initially became worse when I entered spiritual warfare. There have been many days of intense battle as the works of darkness stirred trying to resist the onslaught on "their" territory. But the awareness of becoming progressively freer makes it all worthwhile.

God has used the length and difficulty of the battle to strengthen my spiritual life, to produce patience and endurance, and to tame my formerly selfish and rebellious nature. It has been a source of joy to find myself of more usefulness to God. He has used me in intercession, encouraging others, and praying for their needs, including for deliverance.

"My back is completely healed."

I first realized my need of deliverance when a spirit of infirmity manifested during anointing with oil and prayer for a long-standing back problem. There was an immediate release, but before the week was out, I was in more pain and discomfort than ever before.

Four years earlier I had been baptized in the Spirit, but was never taught about the wiles of our enemy. Within a few weeks, I walked straight into Satan's trap. A chiropractor, who was deeply involved in occult practices and health foods, massaged my back after the birth of our twins, telling my husband that I would recover much more quickly. What a lie! as from then on I had increasing problems with my back and neck. Just as our hands minister the Holy Spirit, his hands ministered demon spirits. Every area he massaged was under bondage to infirmities, inflammation, and pain, and it wasn't till I renounced this association with the chiropractor and had much prayer for deliverance that I was freed. Praise God today my back is completely healed and without pain.

It had been suggested that maybe my whole problem was psychological and that demons weren't the answer at all. But after the demons caused my back to arch unnaturally and let out bloodcurdling screams when the name and blood of Jesus were used against them, it was quite evident what the source was!

As time went on, I learned much more about deliverance, and realized that I needed deliverance in many other areas of my life. My husband and children also experienced deliverance.

Our eleven-year-old son was having a day a week off school with migraine headaches and after prayer for deliverance at a public deliverance meeting, the demon afflicting him left and he hasn't had any headaches since.

We have eight-year-old twin boys, and about eighteen months ago one was very loving and would hug us at every opportunity, but the other was standoffish. After prayer for deliverance from spirits of rebellion, he changed dramatically. He has become so loving that it is now difficult to put them to bed at night because they both want to hug and kiss me at least a dozen times. I thank God for discernings of spirits which reveals the source of our many problems.

A lifetime of nightmares broken — Daphne Drummond

To give you some idea of the power that fear had in my life, I will have to take you back to my early childhood. I was born in India where my father was an electrical and consulting engineer. At the time of my birth he had designed and was supervising the construction of an electrical plant for His Highness, the Maharajah of Bikaner. This meant that my parents lived a very social life, and we children were frequently left in the care of the Indian servants.

We were strictly brought up and one of the rules was: to bed at six o'clock winter and summer. At six o'clock in summer, with the sun still up, it was hard for children to go to bed. To make us go, the Indian servants would threaten us: "If you don't get into bed, the jackals or the tigers will get you!" When this did not work, they would hide on the stairway and make animal noises. By this time it was normally dark, and I would spring into bed, pull the sheet over my head and lie still, almost too frightened to breathe. Any minute I expected the tiger to spring onto my bed and devour me. I was petrified. This happened night after night, and my little heart would almost jump out of my body with fear.

If it was not the servants frightening us, it was snakes. We children were not allowed out of bed until our slippers had been searched for snakes and scorpions. Thus at an early age, fear took hold of my life, and as far back as I can remember, I suffered from nightmares.

One day, as punishment for being disobedient, my parents went out with my sister and left me home with the Indian servants. Our bearer went out and came back with an Indian who was brandishing a huge sythe and threatening to kill me. The bearer pretended to struggle with him and eventually got him to go. I froze on the spot; I was terrified; my eyes must have been as large as saucers, and my heart was pounding. The bearer came back with his finger bandaged up saying, "Look what he did to me as I struggled to save you!" I stood, unable to move. Our parents did not know what was going on. We never reported the servants. This we were never encouraged to do.

The fears began to plague me, increasing as I grew older. When I came to Australia at nine years of age, I would not go into a dark room and switch on the light, much to the disgust of my mother's relatives with whom we were staying. They called me a coward. A girl my age too frightened to put on a light!

As I grew up, the nightmares increased. I accepted them as something I could not do anything about. At the age of eighteen, when I became a Christian, I began to pray about the nightmares, never going to bed without asking the Lord to keep me from them, even pleading the Blood upon myself.

As time went on, I felt the call of God to go to China as a missionary. In preparation, I went to Bible School and there the nightmares intensified and became more frightening. Every night I would dream of demons. Some nights they would be sitting on my chest, trying to press the breath out of my body, and saying they were going to kill me. In my sleep I would be paralyzed. Struggling to wake up, there would be a voice within me saying, "The Blood! The Blood!" When I eventually woke up, I would be in a bath of perspiration, my heart pounding, and a physical pain of tension gripping my stomach. These constant dreams left me exhausted. There were times when I sat up late, almost too frightened to go to bed.

Having prayed about it, but still feeling distressed, I talked to one of our pastors who had been used in the deliverance ministry in Scotland during a revival there. He said to me, "Daphne, I guarantee that if you gave up your call to China, got yourself a job, and settled back to ordinary life again, those dreams would cease." Be that as it may, I was setting my goals towards China, and not even these dreams would deter me.

I went to China with the fears still troubling me in my dreams. Many of them were so vivid, I would have to get up, turn on the light, walk about, and wake myself up. Otherwise I would go back to sleep and continue on where the dreams left off. They were draining my strength. Of course, China was no country to cure fears. Before I went, a retired missionary had told me to be prepared to lose everything at least once during my missionary life. They had been robbed of everything three times.

We were "bandit conscious." When leaving us on our own, our superintendent always said, "If the bandits come, don't try to intercept them, let them take what they like. Your life is worth more than money or goods." We used to go to bed with a kerosene lamp and our Chinese dress by our bed in case we had to get up in a hurry. One person was always responsible to be on guard. One of our missionaries was stabbed when trying to intercept bandits.

When I came out of China, having to flee because of the Communist takeover, the pattern of my nightmares changed. Now it was Chinese bandits chasing me. They would be around every corner coming towards me with knives, or down a dark tunnel. It was either bandits or snakes. The snakes were so numerous that I could not tread anywhere without stepping on them. Some were huge, their jaws open within inches of my face, ready to swallow me. I would wake up in a bath of perspiration with my heart racing, and the fear pain in my stomach. It troubled me and I wondered what I could do. I had prayed about it and used the Blood so often, yet nothing seemed to work. I tried to overcome it with all the will power I had, but to no avail.

In 1977, after many years home in Australia, I moved to another city, not knowing what God had for me, and was quite surprised when the door opened and I was plunge into the ministry of deliverance. Pastor Graham Powell approached me and invited me to join him when praying for women. He had been praying for someone to join him, and my name had come to his mind. This is how God began to teach me, and I here wish to thank God for Pastor Powell's ministry and all He taught me through him.

One day I happened to mention that I was plagued with nightmares; so Graham offered to pray with me. He began to pray against spirits of fear. As he prayed I felt absolutely nothing. There were no manifestations, but Graham said he saw spirits leaving me.

Three times he prayed for me, and after that I was on my own. When I was traveling on the bus, I would often use the minutes to command the demons of fear to leave. Just quietly under my breath I would command them to leave in the name of Jesus. It was an exercise of faith, because I did not feel anything stirring inside, nor did I have any outward indication that they were leaving.

At first I did not understand why it was necessary to keep on daily commanding. Previously, the only understanding I had of deliverance was what I had seen a few times at altar calls, and read about. The idea had formed in my mind that they came out at the first command, and you were then free.

However, I had an open mind to the new things I was learning — and there was much to learn. In faith I continued commanding them to leave. After a while I began to notice that the nightmares were becoming wider apart. I might go for two weeks and not have any.

The question is often asked: "How do you know when you are delivered?" How do you know when you are well when you go to a doctor? By losing your pains and aches and symptoms. I watched the "symptoms" become less frequent and less violent in nature, and it was by this that I knew God was delivering me. It is good to stop now and again, and look back and see how far the Lord has brought you. You see a big change.

Still I kept on, and it did not take long to learn that there is not

198

only one demon to drive out, but many. At first I could not understand this, but now I know by experience. They do not come in by ones, but by many. They set up quite a colony — even in one area — and it is "demons" you are dealing with, not just "a demon."

I constantly commanded in *faith*, not feeling anything; but it was evident that something wonderful was happening. I was waking in the morning not feeling worn out. It was marvelous to get a good night's sleep after years of waking up feeling I had not gone to bed. At the end of about three months, the nightmares ceased, and what a joy filled my heart to know that deliverance is for today and is real. I might add that towards the end I began to yawn a few times. This was the first outward sign I had had that the demons were leaving me.

Our total redemption for spirit, soul, and body was won on Calvary. If we receive salvation by faith, then deliverance is by faith too. It is part of Jesus' great commission in Mark 16:15-18. First to preach the gospel (salvation), second to baptize (water baptism), and third to cast out demons (deliverance). It is God's desire to see His people free, and it can be a reality. God has given us the "keys of the Kingdom." *Faith* turns the key. I found that God was putting the "key" into my hand, saying, "Deliver yourself," and I had to rise up and use it.

Because I knew so little about deliverance, I began to search the Word with an open mind and many scriptures opened up to me. They became quickened to my heart by the Holy Spirit and these I used in faith. As time went on, my faith began to grow and I was being launched into a deliverance ministry for other people. Demons are real — and so is deliverance. God is still on the throne. *Faith* brings God into action, and demons flee before His presence.